THE FAMILY FREEDOM CHALLENGE

"Replaced my income, quit my full time job, and then retired my husband."
—Heather

THE
FAMILY
FREEDOM
Challenge

HOW MAMA BEARS ARE BECOMING
MILLIONAIRES LEVERAGING THE
ONLINE ECONOMY

CHELSEY & STEPHEN DIAZ
FOUNDERS OF *THE RAINMAKER FAMILY*

The Family Freedom Challenge
© 2023 by Chelsey and Stephen Diaz
FamilyFreedomBook.com
TheRainmakerFamily.com

This title is also available in Kindle format.

Back cover photography by Jordan Galindo www.jordangalindo.com
Interior by Kent Avenue Photography www.kentavenuephotography.com

ISBNs:
979-8-9884764-3-6 The Family Freedom Challenge HARDBACK
979-8-9884764-4-3 The Family Freedom Challenge PAPERBACK
979-8-9884764-5-0 The Family Freedom Challenge DIGITAL

Printed in the United States of America

Disclaimer: The sales figures stated in this book are personal sales figures and Rainmaker Family LLC student's personal sales figures. Please understand our results and our student's results are not guaranteed. We are not implying you'll duplicate them (or do anything for that matter). We have the benefit of practicing passive income generating techniques for 7+ years and have an established skillset as a result. **Information without action is worthless**. If you invest in any Rainmaker Family LLC information and do not take action you will get little to no results. We use these real and verified references from real students for inspirational purposes only. Your results will vary and depend on many factors... including but not limited to your background, experience, and especially work ethic. All business entails risk as well as massive and consistent effort and action. If you're not willing to accept that, please return this book or give it away to someone else. Thank you!

DEDICATION

We dedicate this book to our sons Kaizen Shine & Oliver Wave. You were the reason we took the risks, made the leaps of faith, and powered through any walls that came up along the way. The depth of love we have for you is beyond measure. You have taught us to have an abundant mindset, and we know you'll carry on our legacy of generosity and the resourceful "How can I?" mindset in all things.

To all of the mamas who know you are made for more. . . you may be sitting on the bed nursing your baby, running the household, or in a current career pathway... we see you. We know you're working hard to raise world changers. We believe in you and pray this book is a massive step in the right direction towards creating generational change.

Your mindset, growth, and financial abundance when you choose it will be more than you could have hoped. You are wired for this and capable of great things!

CONTENTS

SECTION ONE

Get Ready

To upgrade your experience,
take our virtual 7 day parallel training
that mirrors this book:

www.rainmakerchallenges.com/book

—

For more information of how we can help
reach goals of time & financial freedom,
this book includes 1 complimentary strategy
call with our team of abundance advisors,
watch the case study and book your call here:

www.rainmakerchallenges.com/apply

HOW TO USE THIS BOOK

What would it be like for you, if you could wake up *every* morning feeling excited and energized to work on something that has the potential to change your life and your family's future forever?

Imagine having the power to create a passive income stream from home... That's exactly what The Rainmaker Family is all about.

For several years, we've hosted these challenges for motivated moms who want to create additional income streams from home.

People from all over the world have joined us for our Rainmaker Challenge, and we're honored and thankful you've chosen to work through the book version of our challenge.

This is not just any book. This is a CHALLENGE that will take you on a journey of discovering whether creating an online passive income stream is something you're wired for. We want to tackle the biggest questions you have, just like our live challenges do.

Before you dive in, let us tell you a secret. **The key to your success is making a powerful choice RIGHT NOW, to commit to this challenge.**

Are you ready to take action and see amazing financial results, or is this just another good idea that will fade into oblivion through inaction?

We've seen thousands of moms go through our challenge, and we know it produces "good fruit". Our goal with this book is to produce *results* because good trees produce good fruit.

We believe you are good soil, and when we plant all this information in you, it's going to grow up to be something amazing and change your life like it did ours.

But we don't want you to just read this challenge passively. We want you to **actively participate** in the learning experience.

In Section One, you'll hear our own story, and learn a concept that has changed our lives called "The Four Levels".

Section Two is where your 7-day "Rainmakers Challenge" officially begins.

We recommend **reading one chapter from this section per day for seven days**. Each of the seven days will have a bit of homework for you. We call it getting your "quick win" for the day. It's going to take you step-by-step towards the goal of launching a passive income business. The further you make it in the challenge, the more amazing information and tools will unlock!

But it's not just about the information and tools. Along the way, we'll share stories from real moms and dads who are experiencing life-changing financial results with their Amazon businesses. You'll also have access to bonus information, special resources, videos, and other helpful items.

In Section Three, we'll give you helpful **next steps** for your business-building journey.

You'll learn about how you can join us in one of our upcoming live challenges online and more about our Rainmaker Mastermind, which is for those who complete the challenge, do all their "Quick Wins," and want the fastest path to launching and scaling a "hands off" revenue stream for their family.

Our sincere hope is for you to catch the vision, creativity, and strategy contained within this challenge:

Vision – that you CAN do this, and it can work for YOUR family too, just as it has for countless others...

Creativity – realizing the many potential options and ideas that can fit your goals and personality...

Strategy – the best practices, tools, pitfalls to avoid, and a tried-and-tested step-by-step path to success!

So, what would it be like for you, if you could wake up every morning feeling excited and energized to work on something that has the potential to change your life and your family's future *forever*?

Are you ready to take the challenge and jump all in? Grab a pen, a highlighter, a notebook, or whatever you need, and let's do this thing! See you on the other side!

—Chelsey and Stephen Diaz, *The Rainmaker Family*

OUR STORY

Are you tired of the daily grind, working long hours just to make ends meet? Are you longing for financial freedom and the ability to live life on your terms?

Well, we've got a few secrets to share with you about how we make passive income and how we've helped thousands of others do the same.

But before we get to that, let us tell you our story. It's important for you to know why we're doing this and how we got started.

We're passionate about creating passive income and financial freedom for ourselves and others, and we're excited to share our journey with you. We want to help you avoid the same mistakes we made so that you can reach your financial goals faster.

We've experienced firsthand the power of mentorship and learning from those who have gone before us. That's why we want to be your mentors and share with you everything we've learned along the way.

We believe that when one person succeeds, it empowers and inspires everyone else to succeed. That's why we want to help you reach your breakthrough, just like our mentors helped us reach ours.

We'll share both the awesome results and the not-so-awesome details because we believe that avoiding mistakes and saving yourself pain is just as valuable, if not more, as just learning the tips and strategies.

So get ready, because we're about to take you on a journey that will change your life forever!

OUR BUSINESS BACKGROUND

Are you tired of feeling stuck in a job where you're just trading your precious time for a paycheck? We know that feeling all too well.

We were once in the same boat, running a wedding photography and videography business and feeling like we were hitting a ceiling. We dreamed of growing our family and not missing out on precious moments with them, but we couldn't see a way out of trading dollars for hours.

That's when we decided to start looking for other ways to make money passively, without having to trade our time for every dollar. We tried all kinds of things, experimenting with selling on eBay, dabbling in Airbnb and other rental services, and making both short and long-term investments.

In those "spaghetti years" (just as Stephen likes to say) it felt like we were throwing spaghetti against the wall, to see what stuck.

Yet nothing really clicked until we stumbled upon this little-known way of selling products on Amazon. It blew our minds and changed everything for us. With Amazon FBA, we started small with our first product, the Kururin.

Stephen saw it blowing up on Amazon so we decided to launch our little wooden toy on Amazon right around that time, and Kururins got featured on Mashable shortly after. Because of this media attention, we started selling $600 a day in these little wooden toys. It was crazy! We remember being at a wedding, sweating in the heat of the summer. We had a break to eat at the reception and looking down at our phone and seeing money come in passively, it was a game changer. From then on we were hooked and knew we had to replicate this success.

(Thankfully now we've developed a step-by-step system to look at sales data BEFORE we take risks on products to sell, so we can make educated product decisions. We're no longer winging it and hoping for the best anymore. We'll share more about that later.)

Now, we're able to live the life we've always dreamed of, with the freedom to spend time with our family and work on the things that truly matter to us. We want to share our journey with you and help you shortcut your path to financial freedom.

We hope that this book will help you avoid the "spaghetti years" and give you the tools to succeed on Amazon without the risk and uncertainty we faced. It's time to release control, invest in yourself, and see what can happen when you stop trading dollars for hours.

A FREEING NEW MINDSET

We know what it feels like to be drowning in work, trying to do it all and feeling like you're running in place. We've been there, doing 43 weddings in a year with back-to-back shoots, editing, and travel. It was exhausting, and we were barely able to keep up. But we kept pushing, hoping that somehow we would be able to break through and achieve our goals.

Then we had a breakthrough: outsourcing. It wasn't an easy decision, and we were afraid to let go of control at first. But we realized that we couldn't do everything ourselves, and we needed help. So we took a chance and hired someone to help us with our editing. And you know what? It was a game-changer!

Suddenly, we had more time and energy to devote to other areas of our business and our life. We were able to explore new opportunities and avenues that we didn't have time for before.

And the best part? We started making more money. That's right! By out-sourcing and freeing up our time, we were able to create more income streams and grow our business.

And here's the thing: you can do it too. Whether you're a stay-at-home parent or working a nine-to-five job, outsourcing can be a game-changer for you. It's all about having the right mindset and realizing that the investment you make in outsourcing will pay off in dividends. When you spend a little money on outsourcing, you're buying back your time, which is priceless.

We share this because we get it - you may feel like you don't have a ton of time, which is exactly where we were. However when we "bought back our time" through outsourcing, we freed up our time to end up making more money! Are you open to outsourcing?

Here's the key: Have the mindset that when I spend $15 on this thing/service, it's going to pay me back because it frees up my time to give myself a raise by doing more valuable tasks or spending my time on more valuable things (like being with my family).

So, are you ready to take the leap and outsource? We understand that it can be scary to let go of control and spend money on something new. But trust us: it's worth it. By outsourcing, you'll be able to focus on the things that matter most to you, whether that's spending more time with your family, pursuing your passions, or growing your business.

Don't let fear hold you back from achieving your dreams. Embrace this new mindset of valuing your time over money, and watch your life and business flourish.

3

THE FOUR LEVELS

Imagine you're working hard on your business, but no matter how much effort you put in, your income stays the same. You're stuck in a rut and can't seem to break through to the next level. It's frustrating, right?

That's exactly where we were until we learned about The Four Levels.

As we were sitting in the audience at a marketing conference, a man walked up to the stage named Myron Golden. When he opened his mouth, what we are about to teach you came out. As we scribbled notes, there was something inside us that said, "This will change you forever".

We were blown away by this concept because it's so simple, yet incredibly powerful. It has transformed the way we approach our business and helped us find our direction. We're confident that it will do the same for you.

So grab your pen and paper, take notes, and get ready to LEVEL UP. The Four Levels is a compass that will guide you to success.

It all starts with the basic understanding that money follows value. **The more value you offer, the more money you make**. It's that simple!

MONEY FOLLOWS VALUE

Think about it, the biggest companies in the world, like Amazon, Uber, Apple, and Tesla, are successful because they offer tremendous value to their customers. They solve big problems and make their customers' lives easier. And because of that, they make a ton of money. If you can offer more value to the marketplace, you can increase your income too.

But here's the catch: **many people get stuck at Level One.** They work hard, but they're not offering enough value to break through to the next level.

But here's the thing: many people default to Level One, which has a ceiling and limits your income potential. We started there too, but The Four Levels has given us the tools to break through that ceiling and offer more value.

We're excited to share these levels so you can start offering more value, making more money, and leveling up your business. Grab your notes and highlighter because you won't want to miss this.

Let's dive in and start leveling up!

LEVEL ONE

Level One is implementation.

Have you ever felt like your income is limited by the number of hours you can put in? Have you ever felt like there has to be a better way to make more money without sacrificing your time and energy? We felt the same way when we were wedding photographers. We were stuck in Level One, where we were the ones doing the thing, and our income was limited by how much time we could physically put in. It wasn't until we learned about the other levels that we realized there was a way to break free from this cycle and create more value for ourselves and others.

The income range for people on this level is minimum wage to about $80,000 on the high end. These are just broad averages. Some specialized skill sets may make a little bit more than this (ie: a brain surgeon), but the key thing to know about Level One is it means **you are the person who does the thing.**

Level one is where many people start, and there's nothing wrong with that. But if you're ready to level up and make more money, it's important to understand that there are other levels to explore. When you can offer more value to the marketplace, you can increase your income. We learned this the hard way, by hitting the ceiling of Level One and realizing we needed to find a way to scale our business without sacrificing our time and energy.

As you know, we were wedding photographers. We were the people doing the thing, using our hands, clicking the shutter button, shooting the weddings, editing the photos. Our income was limited by how much time we could put in. Since we were the only people doing the thing, we could only give so much value to others. We could only solve small problems, serving clients one by one. One bride here, one bride there, one wedding a weekend. We couldn't multiply ourselves.

Yes, we could make a lot of money doing the thing, and we were able to scale that business by giving away more of our time, but our income had a ceiling. We only had so much time. As we dreamt about having a family, we knew we needed to buy back our time a little bit and step away from being the people always doing the thing.

So if you're tired of feeling like you're stuck in Level One, like you're limited by the number of hours you can work in a day, there is hope. We've been there, and we want to share what we've learned so you can skip the struggle and start creating more value for yourself and your family.

LEVEL TWO

Next is Level Two, where you start stepping into unification. This is where you are the person who *manages the people who do the thing*. The income range in Level Two is on average, between $40,000 and $250,000.

Totally miraculously, we sort of fell into Level-Two thinking. This wasn't our default way of thinking about business. Being on Level Two was a dream we had, but we didn't know what to do or how to make the shift. Then, a divine opportunity was suddenly thrown in front of us.

Along with photography, we were doing videos. We shot a documentary for a healthcare company, and they loved this documentary. So much so in fact, they asked, "Hey, can you make a documentary for all of our facilities?" All of their facilities totaled 75 all over California and one in Texas. Oh my gosh, that was crazy, and we really wanted that job. As we did the math, we'd have to travel a lot, and it would take six years. Yikes. Of course they would want it done faster...

We took a chance and sent an email with our bid for the job attached saying we could do this by assembling a team and get it done in six months. To our surprise, ding! We got an email back. They signed the contract! We said, "Okay, let's go, let's do it."

This was a $225,000 project! We usually made a few thousand dollars on video jobs, so to have a signed contract with a $225,000 budget blew us away.

It was exciting, yes, but we had no idea how we were going to make this happen. We just threw it out there on a whim. There was no team, so it was time to scramble, but sometimes growth comes from uncomfortable steps. It's like going to the gym. You're not actually growing muscle unless you push yourself until muscle fatigue or failure, right? That might not be the perfect analogy, but the same concept rings true. You have to push yourself, and stretch yourself.

So with our leap of faith out there, this company took it. They said, "Yes, we'll do that, let's do this thing." Their yes, forced us to think *how can we?*

It's very tempting when you have big opportunities like this to say, "No, I can't, I can't." Remember this as we get into day one, day two, or day three of the challenge. You might be thinking *I can't* at times, but we want to encourage you to trade that mindset this week with this instead: **"How can I?"**

Because we changed our thought process to *"How can I?"* with that one job, we were able to step into Level Two, increasing our income without increasing our time investment.

Stephen went to town messaging a bunch of his friends from film school. Since school, they had spread out, and we were able to develop a network all over California so we could cover each of the facilities.

We gave them $1000 per job and the best part of the story is leveling up meant we were able to pay our friends over $100,000 that year!

Then, it became about handling the editing. If we were going to edit all of the videos ourselves, not only would it drain all of our time, but it would also be painful editing the same type of project over and over and over again.

Stephen found an editor by posting in a Facebook group and he loved the job opportunity. He handled all of the editing and made $500 per project, earning over $37,500 to be the person who did the implementation (editing).

That year, we unlocked an additional $87,000 just by managing this project, and setting up the system. We shipped hard drives to the filmmakers, scheduled the shoots, gave them a shooting guide for consistency, and then had them ship the drives to our editor who put it all together and delivered them to the client.

We increased our income, simply by managing the people who did the thing.

When we leveled up from Level One to Level Two, we sat at a desk just making sure the system ran. This leveled up our thinking. "Wow, Level Two, we can manage the people."

Level Two requires using your management skills to unify people, and create systems to save you time. **When you can save time and multiply yourself, you can offer more value to the marketplace, therefore increasing your income.**

Can we tell you a secret? This challenge is simply about this: leveling up from Level One to Level Two. Did you know Amazon is the easiest platform that allows everyday families to move up to Level Two? Amazon has all the resources: a bunch of warehouses, thousands of employees, trucking systems, logistics, robots, and maybe even some drones.

In this book we'll show you the way we've used their people, systems, and resources to grow our passive income, and how you can too.

Now, if you have a lot of questions about Amazon right now, it's okay. On day one of the challenge tomorrow, we'll break down exactly what we're talking about and how you can use this system too.

In short, we teach you how to utilize Amazon's resources to sell products passively. **You are the person who manages the people who do the thing.** You pay Amazon a small fee and they handle the shipping, the customer service, and everything for you. That's where this business truly becomes passive.

At Level Two, you still may do some Level One tasks, but you start managing people who do the lower-paying tasks so you can focus on higher-paying tasks. When we made this shift, our income increased significantly. We were able to outsource and buy back our time piece by piece, so we didn't have to hustle ourselves into the grave.

We also learned the importance of WORKING FROM REST. Rest is crucial to being productive and successful in life, and it's where you can see fruitfulness in your life. By advancing to Level Two, you buy back more time, which allows you to start doing Level Three and Level Four activities sooner. That's when you can start pursuing your dreams and mission and deeper things in your heart.

Are you ready to level up? Don't settle for Level One when there's so much potential for growth and income. Level up to Level Two and beyond!

It's time to prioritize your time and your value so you can create a life and business that you love.

LEVEL THREE

Level Three is communication. This is where you use your words to create wealth, and that's exactly what we're doing with this book. But here's the key thing to remember: these words are *not* just about you.

Because these are the Four Levels of Value, when you offer true value to other people, the primary focus is not on you. Interestingly though, it brings value back to you. To give is to receive.

This is what we're doing with our written communication right now. We are teaching you how to level up, and our words will unlock wealth for you when you partner them with action.

Level Three's income range is $250,000 to $10 million. Examples of people on this level are actors, singers, course creators, consultants, YouTubers, podcasters, and anyone who is training the unifiers to manage the implementers. We want to train you to communicate, unify, and manage the implementers too.

When we launched The Rainmaker Family, we launched it to our "warm audience" of friends and family. But like anyone who has tried launching a business knows, when that dries out, it's where the rubber meets the road. If you truly believe in something, you have to invest in it.

When we launched the second time to a colder audience, we spent $10,000 the first month just to get people on a free training to show them what we learned. Why? Because we believe in this message so much. We want to help change people's lives and they wouldn't hear about it without advertising.

Let's go there for a moment... Facebook ads. We know, we know, just the mention of Facebook ads brings out the haters! We totally get it, and we welcome some skepticism. This book brings people through a process and it's okay to be skeptical of what you see online. There's a big difference between skepticism and negativism though. Negativism says, there's no way this will work, I won't even try it. Skepticism says, this sounds interesting, I will investigate, take action and find out for myself. We have many Rainmakers who are now making money for their families, but at the beginning when they saw a Facebook ad from us, they said, "I thought this was a total scam."

When we talk about how we love teaching others what helped us experience financial breakthrough we often get this question: "Oh, if you're making so much money with Amazon, then why do you charge to teach other people how to make money on Amazon?"

This brings us back to our Level Three discussion – bringing value through communication. It comes down to value. Can we talk with you heart-to-heart for a second? This is a serious topic, and I know some people who read this and see our programs online will have this question.

Here's a practical example: on Amazon, one of our products is called a shirt stay. At a wedding, a friend who is in law-enforcement was wearing one of these little garter things with straps that connected to the bottom of his dress shirt.

"What are those?" I, Stephen, asked. I was kind of poking fun as we got dressed for the big day. He said, "Oh, these are awesome, it's a cop thing. They keep your shirt tucked in because you have to have your shirt looking nice all the time in my line of work. They look a bit funny, but they're awesome. You should try them!"

Hmm...okay, that's actually a good idea, I thought. Since we were shooting weddings at the time, I was always reaching up really high and hanging dresses, etc. My shirt was always coming untucked and looking sloppy!

So, I bought a pair of shirt stays on Amazon and they changed my working wardrobe. They worked so well, but there was room for improvement for sure. I innovated on the design, found a manufacturer and then started selling our own shirt stays on Amazon. Turns out, they were great sellers!

When we sell a shirt stay to let's say, a law enforcement officer, how much is that *worth* to that person? How much value is it for them? True, it does solve one of their major clothing problems, but it's only worth fifteen dollars of value. That's what the market has determined. So they trade us fifteen dollars for these shirt stays, and that's the exchange of value for that item.

In contrast, when we teach someone how to change their life with the same system that changed ours, inside this seven-day challenge, it can change their entire family's finances forever.

How much is that worth? It's certainly worth a lot more than shirt stays. So on Amazon, we're offering a little value to many people, and that adds up for sure. But when we are using words to create wealth here, it's much more valuable, and that's why we get paid more to do this. The fact is, Amazon feeds our bank account; it's something we still actively invest in and grow regularly. And we LOVE how passive it is. However, what we do here feeds our souls.

When we see other families, stay-at-home moms, or people who are struggling with poverty step into financial freedom, that fires us up. The two of us get so excited and even emotional at times about this! We've received Christmas cards in the mail saying things like, "My family was able to go on extra vacations, creating amazing memories with one another this year because of you," "My family was able to buy our dream house because of you," or "I was able to quit my full-time job as a nurse to stay home with my newborn because of you."

These are real stories from people who've gone through the same content in this book. Success stories like this are why we do what we do, and it comes down to offering a higher level of value. Our heart is to see you have results.

We hope you value this training, and that you'll come back to us at the end of this book and say that was the most valuable experience you've ever jumped into!

LEVEL FOUR

Now for Level Four. Let's just cast the vision here, but remember, don't try and jump immediately to Level Four. The people on Level Four are the big dreamers of the world – the Walt Disneys, the Steve Jobs, the Elon Musks, you know?

These are the visionaries, who were crazy enough to take action on a big dream to see it become a reality. At this level, the income range is one million to billions plus. The potential here is unlimited. Honestly, I believe we have some future Level Four thinkers reading this book and in our Rainmakers community right now.

If you have a great imagination, big dreams in the world, or like to solve big problems; this level is for you. At Level Four you leverage ideas to create wealth. You come up with an idea, and all you do is share that idea with your communicators (Level Three), your communicators train the unifiers (Level Two), and then the unifiers manage the implementers (Level One).

It's like when Elon Musk wanted to make a flamethrower. He simply says, "I want to make a flamethrower, that sounds cool" Then, he passes the big idea to his team who does all the rest, right? He's not personally welding together prototypes or going to buy flamethrower fuel. That is Level Four: **you come up with ideas and your team handles those things**. Amazing!

FIRST THINGS FIRST

First though, let's take you through the process of going from Level One to Level Two so you can start freeing up your time, and then you can start moving into Levels Three and Four with the extra time freedom you have. Are you ready to level up? I picture you like Super Mario right before he eats the little mushroom, and then he LEVELS UP.

That's happening for you right now if you've made it this far in our book; **you're leveling up in your mindset so that you can level up in life.**

There's nothing wrong with being an implementer, a doer. In fact, we still trade some dollars for hours in various ways in our business doing some tasks. But it took a mindset shift, to learn to free up our time.

Reading *The Four-Hour Work Week* by Tim Ferris opened our eyes to the idea of outsourcing tasks and acting more like a CEO and less like an employee.

Even with video editing, we held onto doing it ourselves for way too long. "Oh my gosh, I need to be the editor of this video because I am the best editor..." Nope, not anymore!

Instead, we started working with other people and *using our words*, our training, our highest and best use of time to create wealth. We used our words to communicate to the editor we hired how to edit in our style.

It took some time, and it took some patience, but we found editors who regularly work with us and edit all of our videos now. Thankfully we're not sitting here all day editing anymore; we're now pursuing our passion. Our time is freed up to spend more time with each other and our family. Leveling up ultimately led to us being able to start our family, and have our son while still thriving in business and loving every second.

4

TODAY'S YOUR DAY!

Ready For A Cash Injection This Week?

Picture this: You're at the end of your life, looking back at the choices you've made.

You're faced with a decision - do you wish you had focused solely on being an incredible Rockstar mom who raises world changers... or do you wish you had built an amazing business that leaves your family with generational wealth for years to come?

What if we told you that you don't have to choose between the two? That's exactly what the Rainmaker Challenge is all about. We've helped hundreds of families **build successful businesses while being amazing parents.**

In this chapter, we're going to give you a crazy quick win that will help you double your money in one day. We call it the "Double Your Seed Money Day", and it involves using Facebook Marketplace to sell items you no longer need, and turn them into seed money for your business.

The first step is to **take a look around your home and garage and identify any items that you no longer need or use.** The average American has over $3,000 worth of such items, so chances are good that you have some things lying around that you could sell.

Here are a few top categories to inspire you: home decor, seasonal items, electronics, clothes, baby items, and sports and outdoor gear. You can also sell other items that might be harder to find, like camping gear. This is your chance to declutter your home and fund your business at the same time.

Next, **list those items on Facebook Marketplace (FBMP)**. Make sure to take good photos and write clear descriptions that will attract potential buyers. Don't be afraid to negotiate on price, but also don't sell yourself short.

Here are some pro tips that will make your items fly off the virtual shelf on Facebook Marketplace:

1. Offer an irresistible price that will make your potential buyers jump at the chance to buy.

2. Stack the value, by offering bonuses like free items or discounted shipping.

3. Make it easy for your buyers by offering convenient payment options and easy pickup or shipping.

4. Speak to the buyer's desires by creating a catchy caption and engaging post that appeals to their needs and wants.

5. Last but not least, take quality photos in good lighting and with a clean background to show off your items in the best possible light!

Once you've sold your items, take the money you've earned and invest it in your business. This seed money can help you get your business off the ground and begin building generational wealth for your family.

Now, we know that selling items on Facebook Marketplace might not seem like the most glamorous or high-value use of your time. After all, we've just taught you the Four Levels of Value, where the more value you offer to the marketplace, the more income you can make.

But sometimes, you need to start small and build your way up! By getting a quick win like doubling your money on day one, you'll gain confidence and motivation to continue on the path to success.

Not only that, the results you're going to get will help the people in your life see that you're serious about this. And that's really powerful!

I know I've seen so many times where people come in this challenge, and they're doing it on their own. Then, they start making money, and their spouse or family members start to take notice and join them as they get excited about what they are doing.

Remember, it's not just about making a quick buck. We believe that money is like a plant – if you nurture it, plant it in good ground, harvest it, and plant it again; you can grow your investment for years to come. And when you learn how to treat money this way, you can create financial freedom for your family and achieve your dreams.

We've seen this method work time and time again, and we want to share our pro tips with you. Offer an irresistible price, stack the value, make it easy for buyers, and speak to their desires. Don't forget to take quality photos – it can make all the difference.

We know you joined this challenge to start a passive income business, and we'll get to that. But this quick win is a great way to build your confidence and create seed money for your business. And if you double your money or more, you'll be entered into a monthly giveaway.

So, are you up for the challenge? Take action now and start listing your items on Facebook marketplace. Don't forget to post in the group with the hashtag **#FBAfund** so we can see your progress and cheer you on.

www.facebook.com/groups/rainmakerchallenge

We believe in you and can't wait to see what you achieve in this challenge!

Rainmaker

#CELEBRATIONS

Now this one is just a warm up... but after completing each Challenge Day in this book you'll find our **#CELEBRATIONS** section.

In this section, we share inspiring stories from Rainmaker Families who have been through the same process you're going through now.

We share these to motivate, inspire and cheer you on to keep going. Many of us grow up in an atmosphere where only negative things are highlighted, and we see the fear of these negative "what ifs" hold a lot of people back. If that's your default right now, no worries. We share A LOT of stories like this to normalize success and rewire your mind over time.

After you read these say to yourself, if she could do it, I CAN DO IT!

Rainmaker Corinne:

"I'm a mom of three kids and when I started Rainmakers I was getting ready to do my youngest's last year of preschool. After the lockdown a lot of things happened with my family including my marriage ending. It was just a lot.

The next year I told myself, 'I got to do this. I have to do this now.' One day it dawned on me that a product that I used with my kids for 10 years was staring me in the face. I launched my first product in the spring and I'm about 16 months of sales now and it's been amazing. In July I went over 1 million in sales for the last 12 months. I'm reinvesting and scaling and in the new year I'mm going to be starting another brand to grow my business even more."

SECTION TWO

The Challenge

To upgrade your experience,
take our virtual 7 day parallel training
that mirrors this book:

www.rainmakerchallenges.com/book

—

For more information of how we can help
reach goals of time & financial freedom,
this book includes 1 complimentary strategy
call with our team of abundance advisors,
watch the case study and book your call here:

www.rainmakerchallenges.com/apply

5

DAY ONE:
EYES ON THE PRIZE

Over the next 7 days, you'll be learning core foundational content from our $7,800 hands-on mastermind, but for just a fraction of the cost through this book!

This book is written in a way that is designed to encourage you to take action because we know that taking action can lead to financial freedom and time freedom for your family. So, set aside the next hour to focus on creating a brighter future for you and your loved ones!

Before we dive into today's content, here are a few key points to note:

1. Day one is definitely the beefiest because we want to lay a solid foundation that we're going to build on for the entire week.

2. We like to think of these seven days as a summer camp experience! In college, both of us were camp counselors. We saw how students arrived at camp nervous and unsure of what to expect. Yet by the end of the week, they had made friends and experienced transformative moments! We believe this is what your week can be like.

3. Our main goal here is to bring you **results**. At The Rainmaker Family, we are all about helping you achieve your goals and succeed in

creating a profitable Amazon FBA business. Our main focus is to provide you with the resources and strategies you need to get real results.

We believe that sharing your daily wins is a great way to celebrate your progress and inspire others in our community. So, we invite you to share your successes with us by posting in our challenge's Facebook group using the hashtag **#familyfreedombook** here:

www.facebook.com/groups/rainmakerchallenge

Let's work together to make it rain and achieve our dreams!

4. As your mentors in this book, we'll not only share our successes but *also* our failures to help you avoid the same pitfalls. We're committed to being real, authentic, and transparent in this process – to mentoring rather than just teaching, guiding you through the challenges we've faced ourselves.

5. Get ready for daily quick wins! Declare this to yourself: "I am going to have a quick win every single day!"

6. Lastly, we just want to be very clear with our intentions here.

As we mentioned, we've taken our core content, our "secret sauce" from our 12-month program, and put it inside this book. The reason we do this is that just as the late Zig Ziglar famously said, we believe that "you can have everything in life you want, if you will just help enough other people get what they want."

Having said that, although we're good at helping families reach six-figure incomes and even seven-figures, we've never seen someone achieve that result in just seven days.

It's essential to understand that the Rainmaker Method isn't a "get-rich-quick scheme" and success will take time! Think of these seven days as a kickstart towards achieving the result you desire in lifetime and financial freedom for you and your loved ones.

We often use the analogy of sampling at a store like Costco to explain how these initial seven days work. When you go to a store and try a free sample of something; then, you end up buying the whole bag? Or when you're at a nice restaurant and the server offers you a couple of samples before you decide on a glass or a bottle of wine? Or even when you try out a gym on a free trial before committing to a membership? These are all examples of sampling experiences.

Through this book, we want you to have a similar sampling experience with our coaching and expertise.

There are three types of samplers we often encounter:

1. Those who already know they are committed to the outcome, and use these seven days as a kickstart to working with us for the long-term.

2. Those who are unsure and want to test the waters before deciding whether to continue working with us.

3. The serial samplers who go from one trial to another without ever committing to any program or business.

We hope that when it comes to building your business, you won't be like the third type of sampler! Instead, we advise you to genuinely give this 7-day program a try, and if it's a good fit for you, let's work together to help you build that 6-figure income and beyond for yourself and your family!

We don't want to waste your time here, so as we embark on this journey together, we strongly encourage you to make sure you're **committed** to giving it your best and seeing if our assistance is the right fit for you.

If it is, we can't wait to continue guiding you on your journey to achieving the financial freedom we know is possible for you. With that, let's embark on this incredible adventure together!

THE POWER OF LEVERAGE

Let me ask you this: What would it be like for you to have the freedom to live life on your terms? To have the flexibility to spend time with your loved ones, travel the world, pursue your passions, and do the things that truly matter to you?

What would it be like to have a business that's not only profitable but also fulfilling, and aligns with your values and purpose?

Throughout this book, you'll hear parts of our story, which might resonate with your own experiences.

We married young and lived in a small, one-bedroom house that we rented from a family friend. Jumping into business right away, despite not knowing much about it, many people questioned our decision. As expected, we struggled quite a bit, and it took us a long time to gain momentum in our business.

From the outside, it seemed amazing, but we were constantly busy and overwhelmed, as our business was like our baby. We worked in the wedding industry and loved it, but it consumed our weekends and left us burnt out. Ultimately, we were trading dollars for hours, and it wasn't that great.

At some point, we hit a wall. We were burned out, and even though we tried raising our prices, we still inevitably felt weighed down from the busyness when we booked more work. On the other hand, during slow months, we worried about when the next paycheck would come.

Imagine feeling like you're just going through the motions, working day in and day out, but not seeing the fruits of your labor... That's exactly where we were - overextended, overworked, and overwhelmed.

Yet one day, we stumbled upon a book that changed everything. It wasn't even about business or entrepreneurship, but there was one quote that spoke directly to our hearts:

"A vine overextended... will just grow sticks."

That's what the book said, and it hit us hard.

We realized that we were just like that vine - growing and growing, but without any fruit to show for it. We had a few wins here and there, but we weren't having the **abundant harvest** we had hoped for.

But the book didn't just leave us there. It taught us that sometimes, you need to trim the vine. You need to cut back the things that aren't fruitful and focus on what is. It's painful, but necessary.

So, we took a magnifying glass to everything we were doing, and realized **leverage** was the missing piece that we needed!

Our photobooth business was limited by our assistant and we could only do one event per weekend. We were investing time and money into these things, but they just weren't scalable without stretching ourselves thin.

We knew there had to be another way to increase our income, without increasing our workload.

So, we embarked on a side hustle journey, trying various methods like flipping couches, Airbnb, affiliate marketing, blogging, selling toys online, short and long-term investments, starting a YouTube channel, and more.

Everything worked to some extent, but none of it was life-changing until... in 2017, we came across information that blew our minds!

Using software, we saw how much people were earning by selling products on Amazon, and it sparked our curiosity! We started researching how Amazon works, and how people made money on the platform.

What we found was that Amazon had a major problem—its rapid growth. Amazon was outpacing all other retailers combined, with one-third of Americans being Prime members. People increasingly preferred shopping online for the convenience it offers.

With around 1,000 warehouses worldwide and 200 million Prime subscribers, it raised the question of where all Amazon's products came from, and we began asking ourselves: What if we could get paid to help supply products to Amazon's warehouses?

For years we thought Amazon was the one selling all the products, but then we found out about their FBA program. When you read FBA in the remainder of this book, know that these initials stand for "Fulfillment By Amazon". Here's how we explain FBA, and whether you like Jeff Bezos or not, put your opinions about him to the side for a second:

If he called you up today and said, "Hey, I have all these resources. I have these warehouses, I've got trucks, drones, robots, etc., and I have hundreds of thousands of employees. I just want to partner with you. Whatever business you have, I would love to be your business partner."... Would you say yes to this opportunity?

Imagine Jeff saying, "Leverage all of my stuff. I have all this stuff and you can leverage it. You can use it for your business for just a small fee!" Well, that's Fulfillment By Amazon. It allows people like you and me to have shelf space at the world's biggest grocery store: Amazon.

FBA allows you to take your product and put it on a shelf in that grocery store, where thousands of people walk by your product every single day. You don't even have to work at the store! When someone buys that product, they'll check out and give it to the person right for you. In other words, FBA means that as a product supplier, Amazon will fulfill your sales orders for you. They'll even process the payment, provide the customer service, AND ship it for you.

When we found this, we realized this is the greatest entrepreneurial opportunity of our lifetime because it allows us to leverage, leverage, leverage.

Leverage is one of the most powerful things, and all the resources Amazon has built are available for you to leverage for a small fee.

Along our journey, as we began experimenting and one day, listed a wooden toy on Amazon – that's when we experienced the power of leverage for the first time.

I, Chelsey, vividly remember the moment:

Stephen and I were at a wedding, and we were starving. As wedding photographers, we often don't get a chance to eat, so when dinner was served, we rushed to a corner to stuff our faces. That's when we checked our Amazon sales for the day and were almost in disbelief because we had made more money on Amazon than we had shooting the wedding!

This was a weight lifted off our shoulders! We knew that we didn't have to book as many weddings as we thought we needed to. We felt a sense of relief, and it was life-changing. We became Amazon evangelists and started telling everyone about this opportunity. This was a game-changing moment for us.

We started earning $100 a day within three months, $500 a day within six months, and $1,000 a day on Amazon in about nine months.

We were making five to ten thousand dollars per week on Amazon while charging only four to five thousand dollars for a wedding which was much harder work.

Building on this game-changing discovery, we set up a system that paid us while we slept, and that's what this book is all about – **creating a system that frees up your time and finances, giving you the ability to dream again.**

Our wooden toy may not have fit the qualifiers we teach now, but it was a blessing that led us to discover Amazon's leverage. We stumbled into this opportunity, but have now learned how to do it in a proven way. We call it our Rainmaker Method so you don't have to go by trial and error with the viability of your products.

With our tried-and-tested system, we want to help *you* do it the right way your first time too.

Imagine being part of a system that connects millions of customers with the products they need. What if you could play a role in one of the most exciting entrepreneurial opportunities of our time?

What would it be like for you if you could join a community of problem-solvers, creating solutions for people all around the world?

The truth is that every problem is simply **a profitable opportunity waiting to be solved**! We've seen how this Amazon opportunity has transformed lives, and we're passionate about sharing it with others.

We know that many of you have big dreams in your hearts, but time and money may be holding you back. We want to help you break through those barriers and empower you to pursue your dreams.

This is about generational generosity and impact. When you can help others and win, that's when you can create the most significant impact. Along with that, this journey is also about showing your kids what's possible!

Imagine inspiring your children by showing them what's possible when you take a leap of faith and succeed in building a business that works for you.

Seeing their parents overcome challenges and achieve their goals creates powerful teaching moments you are not just telling – but actually modeling – for your children!

Remember the quote from earlier, "You can have everything in life you want if you will just help enough other people get what they want."

Let's rephrase that to **"You can win if you will just help other people win."**

Here are the wins in this opportunity:

(Win #1) Amazon benefits from meeting customer demands with more products.

(Win #2) Customers get what they need.

(Win #3) Factories gain Amazon as a new client and additional business.

(Win #4) And **you** succeed, simply by connecting the dots.

This is what our Rainmaker Method is all about: creating **wins** for everyone involved, including you!

WHICH IS MORE VALUABLE: YOUR TIME OR MONEY?

Right here, let's talk about the most valuable resource we have, and that is time.

It's important to have the right mindset around it, because poor people and wealthy people think about time *differently* when it comes to achieving their desired results:

Poor people *extend* time and rich people *compress* time.

Poor people have a desired result in mind, but their direction is unclear. They continue to get sidetracked and extend time. If you want to get to the future you envision faster, you will need to **learn how to compress time**.

In the early days of our business, we had a poor mindset around time. We wanted to deliver a top-notch experience to our customers, and we were spending a lot of time on things that didn't contribute to our desired result.

For example, Chelsey was making handcrafted cards, but it was taking up a lot of her time that she could have been spending on editing photos or reaching out to new clients.

We soon realized we needed to shift our mindset and compress time to achieve our desired results as fast as possible.

One of the first steps we took was hiring a college friend to make those cards for us. It cost us $12 an hour, but it saved us time that we could have spent on things that generated income for us as business owners. We learned that it's easier to make a lot of money in a short amount of time than a little money in a long amount of time.

So, how do you compress time?

First, **focus on the things that will give you the biggest return on your investment**.

Cut out the things that waste your time and don't contribute to your desired result. Poor people extend time by getting distracted by shiny objects and going round and round trying to achieve their goals. Wealthy people compress time by looking for shortcuts and ways to achieve their goals faster.

We believe that people make time for what they value. If you value spending time with your family or doing activities that bring you joy, you'll make the time for it. The same goes for your business. If you value achieving your desired result, you'll make the time for the things that will get you there faster.

Remember, **it's not about spending money, it's about choosing the right things to work on and giving yourself a raise**.

Our goal is to teach you to outsource as much as you can so you can accelerate your success and buy back your time. If you're reading this book, it's because you value time freedom and financial freedom. Your actions show your true beliefs, and if you're committed to creating that time and financial freedom for your family, the information we'll be sharing is for you.

Let's talk about **the Rainmaker Method**, which we'll refer to throughout the challenge:

To find products that pay our family every two weeks from Amazon, we first choose the right "soil" or aisle where there's demand, but not great products on the shelf. This ensures proven demand. Then, we find the product and have it made, place it on Amazon, and connect to Amazon to receive payment. Finally, we enjoy the harvest and repeat the process. This is a cycle that can be repeated multiple times to scale the business.

During the first phase, we recommend **dedicating four to six hours per week to get everything set up**.

After launching a product, the business shifts to a passive mode, requiring only a few hours per week to maintain. It's worth the initial hustle to enjoy the fruit of your labor for years to come.

Realistic timelines for the first phase are <u>one to six months</u>, mostly due to waiting for manufacturers and Amazon. We'll cover ways to compress time in the rest of this book.

The Rainmaker Method involves finding products that are already selling on Amazon, making them better, getting them manufactured, and partnering with Amazon to get paid for connecting the dots.

In summary, our main focus here is helping you achieve leverage and improve your family's bottom line.

This means we need to let go of the DIY mindset and start leveraging resources to make the most of our time. While DIY projects like refurbishing furniture and flipping it can be fun, they're not practical for building a successful business on the side. Your time is valuable, especially if you're already working a job or taking care of your family.

Committing to four to six hours a week for the next six to nine months is a reasonable timeline to get your products up on Amazon and start generating income.

Remember, you don't have to clock in every day, but staying focused on this process will help you achieve your goals.

Tomorrow, we'll introduce you to an outsourcing website where you'll be able to hire people to help you with various tasks for as little as $5 or $10. These "business partners" will help you compress time, freeing you up more to focus on what matters most!

Additionally, we have a special gift for you today: our power profit tool. This tool acts as an accountant in your pocket, running the numbers to ensure your products are profitable.

We'll show you how to use this software on Days 2 and 3 to save time on product research and identify opportunities on Amazon.

Stay tuned!

YOUR QUICK WIN TODAY:
THE 7-LEVELS DEEP EXERCISE

Are you ready to take your first step towards a brighter future and financial freedom?

The quick win action steps we have planned for each day of this book will help you get there.

But it's not just about taking action. You need a strong reason for why you're doing this.

Your inner "why" is what will keep you motivated and moving forward, not just through our seven days together here, but also in every aspect of your life.

Imagine having the freedom to provide for your family and live the life of deep connection, fun, and meaning you've always dreamed of...

It's possible, and you're worth the effort to make it a reality!

Don't let doubt or fear hold you back. Instead, repeat to yourself, "My future is hopeful!" It's time to unlock your created potential and believe in the impossible becoming possible.

If you need inspiration or support, look to the success stories of other Rainmakers and borrow their faith until you have your own.

To help you discover and strengthen your inner "why," we'd like to offer you a quick win today: The 7 Levels Deep Exercise.

This exercise, created by consultant Joe Stump and taught in Dean Graziosi's mastermind group, will give you a clear vision of why you're pursuing this path. Even if you decide Amazon isn't for you, this tool can be applied to any entrepreneurial venture and serve you for life.

So, are you ready to take the first step towards a better future and discover your inner "why"? Let's do this together.

Step 1 is to ask yourself a question and answer it.

For example, here are a few prompts you can choose from:

- Why do I feel compelled to start a business from home?
- Why do I want to do this Amazon business?
- Why is it important for me to have passive income?
- Why do I want more income for my family?
- Why is it important for me to be an entrepreneur?

Recognize the first thing that pops up in your mind or spirit. Level 1 is usually a surface-level answer, but keep asking "why" for each level to go deeper.

Let the exercise flow. Answers may feel a little circular or unclear, but pay attention to the process, and you may be surprised by what you come up with.

Remember that exercises like this may seem silly at first, but they can lead to powerful insights that are emotionally-compelling and will fuel your vision!

Examples

Example 1

Here's an example of my process (Stephen), starting with the question, *"Why is it important for me to be an entrepreneur?"*

Level 1: Because I love working for myself.

Level 2: (Why is it important to me to work for myself?) Because I love being my own boss.

Level 3: (Why is it important to me to be my own boss?) Because it makes me feel like I'm in control.

Level 4: (Why is it important to me to feel in control?) Because I remember a time in my life when I was out of control and felt hopeless. I was seeking something, but wasn't finding it, and explored unhealthy habits. It didn't feel fulfilling; on the contrary, it felt hopeless.

Level 5: (Why is it important to me to feel hopeful?) Because a future without hope isn't worth living for.

Level 6: (Why is it important to me to have a future full of hope?) Because hope is the entrance to faith, and hope for the future is what unlocks impossible thinking.

Level 7: (Why is it important for me to have hope for the future and unlock impossible thinking?) Because I believe everyone has a great purpose for their life, and I know Chelsey and I were wired with the creative ability to shift the impossible into possible.

This exercise took me from "Why do I want to be an entrepreneur?" to a powerful mission statement that's at the heart of why I do what I do. Isn't that cool?

My Level 7 can be changed into a declaration over myself:

I was wired with a creative ability to shift the impossible to possible. I forerun and release breakthrough for others.

Example 2

To show another example, here is Chelsey's - *"Why is it important to me to be a mom?"*

Level 1: "Why is it important to me to be a mom?" - Because I am drawn to legacy.

Level 2: (Why do I want to leave a legacy?) Because I want to leave the world greater than when I entered.

Level 3: (Why do I want to leave the world greater than when I entered?) Because I believe that's what we're called to do.

Level 4: (Why is it important to have a calling?) Because life would feel purposeless without calling.

Level 5: (Why is it important to have purpose?) Because if I don't follow purpose, I miss living my best life.

Level 6: (Why is it important to live my best life?) Because when I'm living my best life, I feel fulfilled.

Level 7: (Why do I want to feel fulfilled?) Because I believe a life that is fulfilled comes through loving others.

Chelsey's declaration statement is:

I believe that my life is fulfilled when I am loving others.

Throughout our years of experience, we have learned that leaning into our gifts brings us incredible fulfillment and leads to massive impact and results.

This is our "why," the driving force behind everything we do. And we want you to experience the same fulfillment and success in your life!

That's why we strongly encourage you to go through this exercise and create a solid foundation for yourself. It's one of the best ways to set yourself up for success, speak life into your business, and eliminate negativity and fear.

We know that fear can hold you back from starting a business, but we want you to know that Amazon or any other opportunity can be the path to success for you.

The key is to set your eyes on the prize, declare it, and kill all the negativity that says you can't do it. You have the power to overcome any obstacle, and we're here to help you along the way.

Stepping into financial abundance starts with planting good seeds in good soil.

Before we dive into the Amazon strategies, we want you to have a strong "why" that anchors you and keeps you moving forward. We want you to feel confident, even if you don't consider yourself super techy or have much money to work with.

THE 7 LEVELS DEEP

Experience

Why is it important for me to:

Level 1

Level 2

Level 3

Level 4

Level 5

Level 6

Level 7

DAY 1
QUICK WIN SUMMARY:
THE 7-LEVELS DEEP EXERCISE

Are you ready to take action and set yourself up for success? Find a quiet place, grab a pen and paper, and let's get started with the 7-Levels Deep Exercise. Follow the steps we've just shown you and dig deep to uncover your "why".

Once you've reached the seventh level, take that statement and turn it into a powerful declaration over yourself. Speak it out loud and believe it with all your heart.

But don't stop there. Share your exercise results with our supportive community by going live or posting in our Facebook group using the hashtags #familyfreedombook #day1.

By declaring your "why" and sharing it with others, you're taking a powerful step towards achieving your goals and making your dreams a reality.

Remember, words have incredible power. Don't let fear or negativity hold you back. Speak life and positivity over yourself and your business. Set your eyes on the prize and declare it boldly. Let's walk your family into freedom!

WELCOME TO THE

Rainmaker Family Challenge!

DAY ONE
Key to Success

Today is where your Rainmaker Journey officially begins! You are going to to learn the **#1 hack** to building a successful business right out of the gate, in less than 60 minutes a day.

Today's Action
Steps:

☐ *Step One*	☐ *Step Two*	☐ *Step Three*
Read **Day One's** training	Complete The **7 Levels Deep** Worksheet	**Go Live** In The FB Group And Share Your **7 Levels Deep** Worksheet, Or **Post A Selfie** With Your Completed Worksheet

Are you ready? Let's get started!

Rainmaker

#CELEBRATIONS

After completing each Challenge Day in this book
you'll find our **#CELEBRATIONS** section.

In this section, we share inspiring stories from Rainmaker Families who have been through the same process you're going through now.

We share these to motivate, inspire and cheer you on to keep going. Many of us grow up in an atmosphere where only negative things are highlighted, and we see the fear of these negative "what ifs" hold a lot of people back. If that's your default right now, no worries. We share A LOT of stories like this to normalize success and rewire your mind over time.

After you read these say to yourself, if she could do it, I CAN DO IT!

Jansen found **hope for her future**:

"Before I found Rainmakers, I was so stuck. I was working three jobs, and I was just in a really dark mental state. I was struggling and was in this sludge. I saw an ad for Rainmakers on September 10th which I will never forget. That day is Suicide Awareness Day. I was in such a dark place and I just felt like it was the universe telling me, 'this is your thing.'

And so on that day one, when we did our seven levels deep, I dreamed. Doing the challenge reminded me how to dream. And it *changed my life that week. It was the first day of the rest of my life. I've made $30,000 in sales, and my goals don't stop there. My seven layers deep is still my why. And my dreams are still happening because of that."*

Advice from Rainmaker Lucy:

"Since sophomore year in high school, I have been a photographer and videographer. I've spent so much of my life building that business, and I never imagined my world without it until my husband and I had kids. That is when my curiosity piqued and a hunger to learn how to make passive income grew. It wasn't until Rainmakers that I realized how possible it was.

For me as a stay-at-home mom and as someone who already has another business going in the background, I can say that this is totally possible. My Amazon business is the thing that I've poured the least amount of my time into, and after one year, we have gone from zero to $80,000 in sales. We can wake up on Monday and choose how we want to spend our days. Before Rainmakers that wasn't possible. We truly can spend our lives together, and I love that I can spend my days with my kids.

I would say that if I have one regret on this journey, it is that I wish I had started sooner. If you feel any kind of curiosity or a feeling of, 'I know this is for me', I would just encourage you to not wait. Those feelings and that tug is there for a reason. You're in the right place. These are people that genuinely care about you, and you won't find another place that's more generous, more caring, or more willing to truly lock arms with you and help guide you on this journey."

Advice from Rainmaker Sherry **who already had an existing business before she found our community**:

"I had over 100 jewelry items on Amazon, and we manufactured them ourselves. I was spread thin, and after going through Rainmakers, I realized I needed to narrow my focus.

Currently, I'm just focusing on two of my best-selling products, honing them and spending my time developing them while building a stronger presence on Instagram and Facebook. However, my caregiving responsibilities for my husband and father, both of whom have dementia, limit the amount of time I have available. Despite this, I'm intentional about doing something every day.

Don't feel like you have to have everything done overnight. I have friends who were able to fast track, but they had the time to do it. Don't compare yourself to others in the group and feel discouraged if they're further ahead. You'll get there, and Amazon isn't going anywhere. You'll learn as you go and discover what works best for you in your season and timing.

I recently spent a week away from it all, and it was amazing to see the money coming in from FBA without any additional effort on my part. It's an incredible business model, and while some people might think it's expensive to use, I'd argue that hiring an employee or dealing with payroll and workers' comp is more expensive. FBA frees you up to focus on growing your brand and niche."

YOUR BONUS SECTION:
THE AMAZON ADVANTAGE

Did you know that there are three fatal flaws that most businesses face... but building an Amazon business can automatically help you overcome them?

As you read the following paragraphs, we want you to feel inspired and empowered to explore the possibilities towards creating a new reality for yourself and your family!

The first is **the lack of proven demand**.

Many businesses fail because they don't have a market for their products or services. They spend a lot of time and money trying to create demand, but they can't seem to attract customers. This is where Amazon comes in. Amazon is like a giant grocery store, with millions of customers going down different aisles, looking for specific products.

Your job as an Amazon seller is to **find the aisles where there's proven demand but limited supply, and to offer better products that meet customers' needs**. With Amazon's massive customer base and trust, you don't have to worry about marketing, advertising, or building a brand from scratch. You can simply tap into the existing demand and supply it with quality products!

The second is **the lack of time leverage**.

Most businesses require you to trade your time for money. You have to be the one doing the work, promoting the business, and handling customer support. This can be exhausting and limit your earning potential.

With Amazon FBA, you can leverage the power of automation and out-sourcing to scale your business without sacrificing your time and energy. **Amazon takes care of the logistics, shipping, and customer support, while you focus on managing your team and growing your business**. This allows you to earn more money while working less, and to create a business that works for you – instead of the other way around!

Now, let's talk about the third – **the lack of ease in handing over your business**, when you are the face of your brand.

The option to build a faceless brand is a huge advantage of selling on Amazon. Unlike other businesses where you have to promote yourself, run ads, and hustle to get customers, Amazon already has the traffic there. People are already searching for products on Amazon, and they trust the platform. So, all you need to do is supply the demand.

This is not to say that you can't build a brand on Amazon. You absolutely can! But the beauty of it is that *you don't have to*. And that's what makes it such a scalable and valuable asset. Because it's built on leverage, it's attractive to investors. **You're building an asset that you can sell at any point.**

Think about it – what would it be like for you to have a business that you can sell for hundreds of thousands, if not millions of dollars?

What would it be like to have an asset that you can scale and cash flow for an investor?

What would it be like to have a business that doesn't require you, that you can step away from and it will continue to grow and thrive?

That's the power of selling on Amazon. And that's what our Rainmakers are doing. They're building businesses that are not only profitable, but also valuable assets that they can sell for a big return on their investment.

Let's bring it all together at this point. We've talked about the three fatal flaws of most businesses - lack of leverage, lack of time leverage, and lack of being a faceless brand. And we've shown you how selling on Amazon solves all of these problems!

But don't just take our word for it... look at the numbers.

Over 50% of online sales happen on Amazon. People are spending billions of dollars on the platform every year.

And the best part is – *you* *too* can be a part of this!

What would it be like for you if:

1. You could have a business that solves all of the problems that most businesses face...

2. You could run a business that is already built on demand, that has time leverage, and that doesn't require you to promote yourself...

3. And you could build a business that is not only profitable but also a valuable asset that you can one day sell for a big return on your investment?

That's what we want for you. And that's why we're so passionate about sharing this opportunity with others!

We've seen firsthand how selling on Amazon can transform lives and businesses, and now we want to help you experience that same transformation!

6

DAY TWO: FINANCIAL LEVERAGE YOUR "BUSINESS PARTNERS"

What would it be like for you if your family could create a legacy of generational wealth – with just one product?

Close your eyes and imagine for a moment that you're holding something that has the power to change the course of your family's financial future for years to come! A product that could ignite your creativity and contribute to society in ways you never thought possible...

Sounds too good to be true? Not for the Rainmaker community. It's a reality they've experienced time and time again, and today, we're going to share with you our secrets to making it happen.

Welcome to our topic of the day: Business Partners.

Get ready to explore all the tools and resources that can help you save time and money, and empower you to make it rain. This is the foundation of the Rainmaker method, a tried-and-tested process for product research that every Rainmaker starts with.

But before we dive into the nitty-gritty, we want to share with you a core belief and mindset philosophy that underpins everything we do. It's about **shifting from a mindset of "I can't" to "How can I?"**

This simple shift in language has the power to transform how you approach life, dream big, and tackle challenges. We all have a default mode of "I can't" language, shaped by past experiences or negative messaging from others. Yet by embracing a "How can I?" mindset, we open ourselves up to a world of amazing possibilities.

Are you ready to learn how to powerfully profit from the start? Today, we're first going to **talk about money and resources in a way that shows you how to set yourself up for success, so that you can create the generational wealth and financial leverage that you were designed to experience.**

Then, we'll **take a deep dive into the world of business partners and explore how they can help you save time and money, as you build something that you truly own.** This is all part of the Rainmaker Method, and we're excited to share it with you.

Let me share a quick story with you: Back when we were trading dollars for hours, we were still the ones doing the work. We had yet to level up to the next stage where we were managing people doing the work. This meant we were limited in how much income we could generate. But then we got approached by a video production company that wanted us to shoot over 60 videos for facilities all over California.

Initially, I, Stephen, said to myself, "*I can't* do this. There's no way I could travel every week, and be away from my family. Chelsey would never get to see me."

But then I thought, "*How can I* make this happen?" I contacted friends from film school to do the shooting and hired an editor to do the editing.

This allowed us to set up a system to manage the people doing the work, and we ended up getting paid a quarter million dollars from that project, and personally making between $75,000 - $100,000. This was game-changing money for us, and **we were able to achieve it by shifting our mindset from "I can't" to "How can I?"** That's the power of the "How can I?" mindset, which is a key belief of Rainmakers!

It's important to recognize that we live in a culture that often focuses on lack rather than abundance. We've been conditioned to think about what we don't have, rather than what we do have. As Rainmakers, we need to shift our focus from limited resources to abundant resourcefulness. This is about shifting from "I don't have" to "I can have" by recognizing and utilizing the resources we do have.

We want to give you a mindset tool that can help you begin to shift from "I can't," to "How can I?"!

It's called **the "How can I" Post-it Pad Method**, and it's something you can easily implement in your daily routine.

All you need to do is write down "I can't ___" at the top of the post-it note and fill in the blank with whatever limiting belief or obstacle you're facing. Then, cross it out and replace it with "How can I ___?"

You may not have the answer right away, but that's okay. Keep the Post-it note somewhere visible, like your desk, computer, or bathroom mirror. This simple act of writing it down and replacing it with a more empowering question can be enough to open up new possibilities, serving as a reminder to shift your mindset from "I can't" to "How can I?" and help you stay open to possibilities throughout your day.

Many of our Rainmakers have been powerfully impacted in their lives and businesses by this tool that effectively trains your brain to focus on solutions, rather than limitations!

THE LIFESTYLE FREEDOM MODEL

Leveraged income is where we use leverage to increase our income without stretching ourselves too thin or spending crazy money. It's about using systems, employees, and technology to manage the people doing the work so that we can increase our income and create financial leverage.

We'll be breaking down exactly how much it takes to start and run a business, but before we do that, we want to help you self-analyze where you're at.

Our Lifestyle Freedom Model exercise is your first step to creating a plan for financial success, and will allow you to take a couple of moments to be truthful with yourself and assess where you currently stand financially.

The graph on the next page compares financial freedom to time freedom. The x-axis represents financial freedom, with low financial freedom on the left and high financial freedom on the right. When you have high financial freedom, money no longer dictates your decisions, and you will have the freedom to bring the dreams in your heart to reality!

In our program, we work with three types of moms, although anyone can benefit from our approach. These three types are:

1. The Hustle Mama: She might be making good money in a corporate career, but she's giving all her time to it and feeling torn because of it. She's low on time freedom and might be thinking, "I don't know if I can be at this job forever."

2. The Boxed Mama: She has a lot of freedom and time, but not much income. She might have put her gifts and talents on the sidelines to raise her family, and while the time with her kids has been amazing, she's bursting to create, contribute, and leave a legacy.

3. The Stuck Mama: She's working two low-paying jobs and has no financial or time freedom. All her money might be going towards bills, and she feels like she's going in a million different directions.

Take a moment to self-assess and identify where you are on this chart. Are you a Hustle Mom, a Boxed Mom, or a Stuck Mom? Be honest with yourself and take the two question quiz. Once completed, put a dot on the chart to show where you are.

LIFESTYLE FREEDOM MODEL

Hustle Mama

Rainmaker Mama

$ Financial Freedom

Stuck Mama

Boxed Mama

Time Freedom

TAKE THE FREEDOM QUIZ

I have a lot of time freedom **YES / NO**

I have a lot of financial freedom **YES / NO**

Time = NO	Time = NO	Time = YES
Financial = NO	Financial = YES	Financial = NO
"Stuck" Mama	"Hustle" Mama	"Boxed" Mama

Our goal is to help you become a Rainmaker Mama with an abundance of time and financial freedom!

THE
Rainmaker
FAMILY

Whatever your situation, we want to help you overcome the challenges you may be facing to achieve financial and time freedom!

Our goal with this challenge is to help you become a Rainmaker Mama - a mom who has the time and financial freedom to pursue her passions by starting a successful home-based online business! We understand that as a busy mom, you may be feeling overwhelmed and torn between your responsibilities and your dreams. That's why we want to guide you towards success and show you the pathway to achieving your goals.

By putting an actual dot on the chart we presented, you can identify where you are currently and where you want to be.

In just seven days, you may not achieve total financial and time freedom, but our goal here is to help you shift from being a Hustle Mama, Boxed Mama, or Stuck Mama, to a Rainmaker Mama.

Imagine being able to pour your heart and soul into raising world changers, while also having the financial freedom to pursue your own dreams... No more feeling like you have to overextend yourself or take on extra jobs just to make ends meet! This is what we want for you, and we believe that with our guidance, you can achieve it.

So why not take that first step towards your dream today? Put a dot on the chart we presented and let us help you move towards becoming a Rainmaker Mama. We're here to support you every step of the way and celebrate your progress along the journey!

PART 1: MAKING MONEY WORK FOR YOU

Do you ever feel like you're struggling to make ends meet or like there's just not enough money to go around?

If so, I want you to know that you're not alone. We've talked to so many people who have been in the same boat. But here's the thing - it doesn't have to be that way. You can take control of your finances and learn how to use money in a way that works for you.

Also, we know how challenging it can be to reach your goals, especially when you feel like you don't have the resources you need to succeed! That's why we want to share some valuable insights with you that have helped us and many others overcome this hurdle here.

We've invested in a lot of masterminds and surrounded ourselves with successful people who have made millions upon millions. Being around them has stretched our mindset and made us realize that success is conta- gious – you just have to be around the right people. If you haven't had the chance to be around such individuals, don't worry. We're here to help you shift your thinking and give you the tools you need to succeed.

One way to do this is to start thinking differently about money. Instead of feeling like there's never enough, start looking for ways to use what you have more effectively. Have you ever heard the saying, "We cannot solve problems with the same thinking we used when we created them?" It's so true! We're here to help you **learn how to use money like a seed, plant- ing it and nurturing it so it can grow and thrive**.

That's why we want to share with you some tips for starting your own Rainmaker journey with abundant resourcefulness instead of limited re- sources. And don't worry, these tips aren't just for people who are completely broke - they can work for anyone who wants to be smarter with their money.

One of our most popular tips is to leverage borrowing, also known as OPM or other people's money. This might sound intimidating, but it's ac- tually a common practice for many successful entrepreneurs. By borrowing money to invest in an asset like an Amazon business, you can start generating income and building wealth over time.

We know that money can be a big obstacle to starting a business, which is why we want to help you learn how to use money in a way that works for you, so that you can achieve the financial freedom you desire!

Here are some incredible options that our Rainmakers have used to start their businesses with little to no money down.

First, there's the option of **finding an investor**. This method has worked wonders for many Rainmakers, including a guy named Michael. When he first went through our program, he saw the potential but lacked the funds to make it happen. So, he reached out to his family members, starting with his dad, and asked if they would invest using the Rainmaker method. Now, his dad gets a cut of the profits, and Michael has done this with three or four people now. He understands that finding someone who has money but no time or interest in doing the work is the key. You put in the effort, and everyone gets paid. Michael has created money out of someone else's money and gone on to do this with multiple businesses.

We recommend doing this for a season to make some money, and once you have some capital, do your own deals so you can keep more of the profits.

The second method is similar to finding an investor: make it rain for someone else. Remember, if you can help others win in life, you will win too. Do you know anyone with a product who's not taking advantage of the Amazon Goldmine? Maybe it's a local mom and pop shop or a friend with a unique crafty thing. You could approach them and show them that similar products are selling like hotcakes on Amazon each month. Offer to help them create a product and sell it on Amazon, and get paid in the process.

Think about it, who do you know who has an audience but isn't monetizing it with a physical product? Michael did this with a friend who was doing a cool, crafty thing on Instagram. They struck a deal to turn that thing into an accessory and are now raking in the cash. The possibilities are endless.

These are just two ways to start your business with $0. You can do it for one product, take the profits from that product, and reinvest it into your own. We know that some of these ideas may seem out of reach, but we want to open your mind to new possibilities.

By the end of our 7 days together here, you'll understand how to make it rain for yourself and others. You'll be amazed at what you can achieve with a little creativity and determination!

In summary, let's do a quick recap of what we covered before we move on to part two of today's training:

1. We talked about shifting from a mindset of lack to one of abundance, from thinking "I can't" to "How can I?"

2. We also identified where you are on your journey towards lifestyle freedom, whether you're a Hustle Mama, Box Mama, Stuck Mama, or somewhere in between... and we're here to help you become a Rainmaker Mama.

3. We showed you two ways to start your Rainmaker journey with absolutely nothing. And when we say "nothing," we mean it loosely because the belief that you have nothing is just an illusion of limited resources. If you tap into your abundant resourcefulness, you can achieve anything you set your mind to!

Now, let's declare a few things together. Say it out loud, even if you're not sure you believe it yet. Your mouth has to say it before your mind can fully embrace it!

Firstly: **"I will no longer let myself be limited by my lack of resources."**

Next: **"I will leverage my abundant resourcefulness instead."** This is a powerful affirmation that acknowledges the abundance that already exists within you.

Finally, our personal favorite: **"There is more than enough time and money for me to do what I need to do."** Say this out loud and feel the weight lifting off your shoulders. This belief is seven levels deep and worth embracing.

Are you ready to move forward with this new mindset of abundance and resourcefulness? Let's go!

PART 2: LEVERAGING YOUR NEW "BUSINESS PARTNERS"

We're not reinventing the wheel on Amazon. Our goal is to find what's already selling and show you how to do the same.

To start, let's think of Amazon like a huge grocery store. Just like every aisle in a grocery store has a title, there are millions of aisles on Amazon that people are searching for. From baby helmets to dog lickpads, people are searching for specific things they want, and that's the aisle they're going down.

Our job is to help you find those profitable aisles on Amazon where thousands of people are searching for products, and then show you proven software that helps you identify the best opportunities. We look for empty shelves that have low-quality products or have no products at all but are in high demand.

These are the three pillars of profitable products on Amazon that you need to filter through every product you're looking at:

1. First, does it sell well?
2. Second, can it compete on the aisle without oversaturation?
3. And lastly, will it make money with a good profit margin of 35 to 55%?

We'll show you exactly how to calculate your potential profit margin with our Power Profit Tool, which we're giving you for free as a gift with this book. It's on a web app called The Rainmaker App, which is full of resources for your Amazon journey!

You'll find that at
www.rainmakerchallenges.com/bookresources

We've invested over $100,000 in this app for our Rainmakers, and you'll get the basic version for free just by investing in your family's financial future with this book.

It's a valuable tool that you'll use during our time together here, so bookmark it as soon as you create an account:

In the app, we have free resources that can help you in your Amazon business, such as Chrome extensions and a 20% off code for Fiverr, a website we use for outsourcing. We also have tools for speeding up videos, Google Trends, and more!

Feel free to explore the app and use these resources to your advantage in the days ahead, however, for now, we want to stay focused by talking about the number one tool you'll need.

> **To get this tool, follow these steps, starting by opening your Rainmaker Web App at**
> **www.rainmakerchallenges.com/bookresources**

Next, go to the resources section of our web app and click on "software recommendations." This tool is what we use in Rainmakers to find profitable products on Amazon.

In fact, this one tool will both save you so much money and make you so much money, we would be doing you a disservice if we didn't recommend it!

Now, we want to be transparent with you. This tool does require an investment, but the company behind it has generously provided an amazing deal just for you as a part of our group. Helium 10 is used by over a million Amazon sellers, but they've given us a special offer. So, if you're serious about building your Amazon business, you won't want to miss this opportunity!

If you're worried about the money, keep in mind that it comes with a 7-day unconditional guarantee. If you decide the tool isn't right for you, you can get your money back within 7 days. So, you have nothing to lose.

In summary, the two key steps you need to take are **getting the Helium 10 Tool** and **downloading the Helium 10 Chrome extension**. These two tools are essential to finding profitable products on Amazon.

Here are these steps outlined visually for you in a graphic here:

Getting to know **Helium 10**

Follow these **seven simple steps** to set yourself up for success tomorrow and throughout the rest of the challenge.

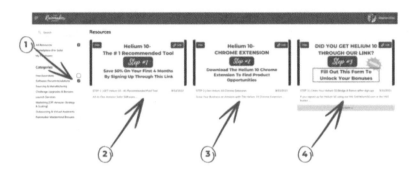

☐ **STEP 1**
Bookmark the Rainmaker app
RainmakerChallenges.com/app

Scan me!

h10.us/UxUb95

☐ **STEP 2**
Get **Helium 10 (Platinum)**
at **GetH10.com**

☐ Open **Magnet** & Find
Your First **TSCRK**

☐ **STEP 3**
Get Helium 10
Chrome Extension

☐ Run **XRAY** (Once) on
Amazon Search Term

☐ **STEP 4**
Fill in **Helium 10 Form**
to get your badge!

☐ Come up with a **list
of things** you could
potentially buy
on Amazon

THE
Rainmaker
FAMILY

Are you excited to learn how to find profitable products on Amazon that could potentially earn a regular income? This is technical stuff, but we promise to keep it simple!

We're going to teach you two essential things right now: how to run Xray and how to find your first TSCRK. Now, I know this might sound like jibber-jabber at first, but it will make perfect sense in the next section.

TAKING A VISUAL XRAY

First, we're going to use Helium 10, a powerful Chrome extension. Follow along with us and search for "baby helmet" on Amazon. We know, it's a funny keyword, but it's a good example for our purposes. These baby helmets look like they're affordable to source and sell for a decent price!

The next step is to learn how to run Xray, which is a tool we've been walking you through. If it's not visible at the top right of your browser, click on the puzzle icon and pin Helium 10 to your pinned extensions.

Note that you don't use Xray on the Amazon homepage. Simply search for a term, even something you've recently bought, and then click on the Helium 10 Chrome Extension at the top. Finally, click on Xray!

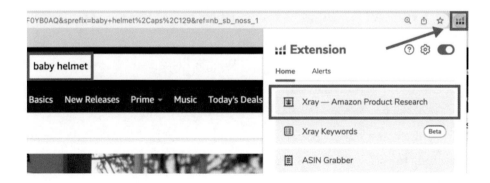

Once you've done that, a new window will pop up.

Tomorrow, we'll show you how to analyze the data, but for today, we just want you to get familiar with the Xray feature. Look around and see what catches your eye. You might notice that the "baby helmet" category has 10,000 searches per month, with a pretty consistent trend over the past year (at the time of writing this).

You can also hover over some of the products to see what they're selling for. Take note of the monthly revenue numbers, like 72,000, 11,000, 45,000, and 142,000. Tomorrow, we'll explain how to qualify if a product is a good opportunity for Amazon.

For now, your homework today is to **search for "baby helmet", click on the Helium 10 Chrome Extension, and then click on Xray to get this window to show up**. If you can do that, congratulations! You got it! As mentioned, in tomorrow's chapter, we'll show you how to analyze the numbers and determine if a product is worth pursuing.

THE "TSCRK"

Let's dive into another important tool that can set you up for success in your home-based online business: the TSCRK, or **Top Searched Closest Related Keyword**. We can't stress enough how crucial this tool is for finding profitable products on Amazon!

Why is the TSCRK so important? Well, it helps you discover the most popular search terms related to your chosen keyword, which can be different from the product you initially had in mind. By finding the top searched keywords, you'll have a better understanding of what people are actually searching for on Amazon, which can help you target your products and listings more effectively.

Let us share with you a personal story about why mastering the TSCRK tool is so helpful, in our experience:

When we were first selling T-shirt stays, which are designed to keep your shirt tucked in, we came across the idea at a friend's wedding. He was wearing them and I (Stephen) was immediately intrigued. Yet when I went home to search for them on Amazon, I had no idea what to type! I started with "shirt tucky thing" but that obviously didn't work. Millions of people are in the same boat, searching for a specific item but not knowing the exact keywords to use.

That's where the TSCRK comes in. We've seen many people struggle with this concept, so we're going to go over it in detail to make sure you understand it well. Trust me, if you can master the TSCRK, you're going to be ahead of the game.

Here's how it works: **To find the TSCRK, click on the "Tools" tab and scroll down to "Magnet."** This is where you'll find the top search, closest related to your keyword.

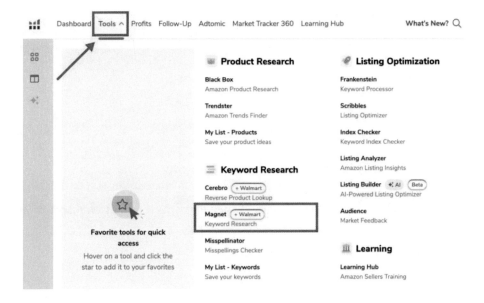

It's important to remember that what you think people are buying on Amazon may not always match up with what they're actually searching for. By using the Magnet tool, you'll be able to understand the search behavior of your target audience and adjust your strategy accordingly. Mastering this tool will set you up for success in the long run!

Let's take the example of shirt stays for men. We'll search for "shirt tucker" in Magnet and sort the results by search volume. We'll then look for the keyword with the highest search volume that is most closely related to the product we're trying to sell, which, in this case, is "shirt stays for men".

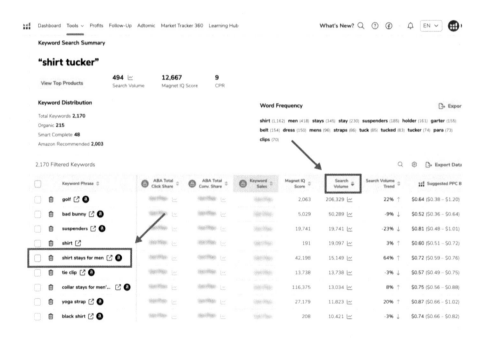

It's important to note that some of the keywords may not be relevant to the product you're trying to sell. So, it's crucial to look for the top searched, closest related keyword to your product.

Let me give you another example. Let's say we're looking for inflatable baby helmets. We'll search for "baby helmet" in Magnet and sort the results by search volume. We'll then look for the keyword with the highest search volume that is the closest related to the product we're trying to sell, which in this case is "baby head protector" at the time of writing this.

By finding the top searched, closest related keyword, we can ensure that our product is placed in the right aisle on Amazon. Placing our product in the wrong aisle can drastically reduce the number of potential customers who see it.

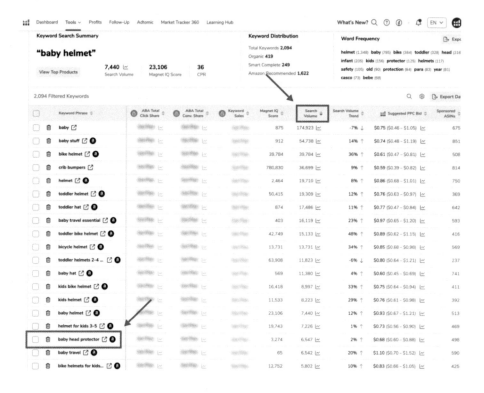

We hope this explanation makes sense to you. We'll be going more in-depth into utilizing your TSCRK tomorrow, but for now, let's just keep it simple and help you focus on mastering the two key strategies we discussed today.

With these 2 powerful strategies in your arsenal, you're on your way to finding the perfect product and achieving success in your soon-to-be Rain-maker business.

YOUR DAY 2
QUICK WIN:
GETTING STARTED WITH HELIUM 10

Are you ready to jumpstart your Amazon FBA business? Then it's time to invest in the right tools. And when it comes to essential business partners, Helium 10 is the number one tool we highly recommend!

Don't waste any more time trying to make it work with free tools that only get you so far. With Helium 10, you'll have access to a comprehensive suite of features that will take your product research and optimization to the next level.

Signing up for Helium 10 is an investment in your future success. This is the #1 tool you're going to need if you're serious about setting up your Amazon business, so go ahead and do it now!

Visit **www.rainmakerchallenges.com/h10bookdeal** to receive 50% off your first four months of Helium 10. We recommend the Platinum plan for those who are just getting started.

You don't have to commit to a long-term subscription, but trust us, you aren't likely to want to cancel it once you see the results. It's a small investment that can pay off big time in the years ahead, plus there's a 7-day unconditional money-back guarantee if you decide this isn't for you!

Helium 10 will help you make money by optimizing your listing and doing email follow-ups. Plus, they have the Refund Genie tool that can help you get back money that Amazon owes you. But don't take our word for it. Be sure to try it out for yourself. Take some of your product or keyword ideas and run them through the tools like we've just taught you!

Once you've done this, join our Facebook group here: **www.facebook.com/groups/rainmakerchallenge** and share your Helium 10 quick win with us in our Facebook group with the #familyfreedombook!

See you on the inside!

Rainmaker Family Challenge!

DAY TWO
Your Business Partners

Today you are going to learn all about the essential product
tools we use to find **profitable products.**

Today's Action
Steps:

☐ *Step One*	☐ *Step Two*	☐ *Step Three*
Read **Day Two's** training	Complete The **Helium 10** Worksheet	Post Your **H10 Subscriber Badge** In The FB Group.

Are you ready? Let's get started!

Rainmaker

#CELEBRATIONS

Rainmaker Heather who didn't feel like she had much time for this:

"When I joined Rainmakers, my daughter was about eight months old and I was working part-time, which didn't leave me with a lot of free time. People often ask me how much time they need to commit to this, and my answer is that it can work either way. If you have a lot of free time, you could spend five or six hours a day and complete the training quickly. Alternatively, if you have a job or children to take care of like I did, you could work on it for an hour or two a day, and that's perfectly fine too. It may take a little longer to get started, but you'll still get there eventually.

If you're worried about not having enough time, it shouldn't be a deterrent. When I started, I spent most of my time researching what I wanted to sell, figuring out a brand name and logo, and placing orders. Despite only spending an hour or two a day, I launched my first product on July 1st, about four months after starting. Waiting for my product to be made and shipped took the most time, with about 45 days for each. In reality, it only took me about a month to decide what I wanted to sell, get everything set up, and have it on its way."

Heather's business has now crossed the $1,000,000 in sales mark putting her in our 7 Figure Family award winner club! Not only did this help her retire from her job to spend more time with her girls, but her husband has significantly cut back on his hours as well after he caught the "Rainmaker Spirit" and launched his own brand on Amazon. We send these gold records out to our Rainmakers when they reach these #celebration milestones.

If you're dreaming of owning a business like Heather, join our Mastermind program where you can work directly with a coach to implement what you're learning in this book and beyond. Book your strategy call with our team to ensure the Mastermind is a good fit for you and your family:

www.rainmakerchallenges.com/apply

7

DAY THREE: FINDING GOLD

Welcome back! Today, we're going to dive into some essential tools that will take you from "beginner to pro" in under an hour. We'll show you how simple it is to **discover hidden product opportunities** that you would never think to sell on Amazon.

Today is all about finding gold - those profitable products that are just waiting to be discovered. Imagine what it would be like if you could look up any product on Amazon and "find gold"? That's exactly what we're going to be showing you with our Rainmaker Method.

To use an analogy, yesterday, we took you to "the gym" and showed you some equipment, and encouraged you that yes, you can do it!

We hope that you've been thinking of potential product ideas and jotted them down.

If you don't have any ideas yet, don't worry! We're even going to show you a way to find those items on Amazon with just a couple of clicks. Remember, it's all about the data. We don't just hope and pray that something works. We take calculated risks, and that's what we do in the Rainmaker Method.

So get your Helium 10 ready because today is going to be a really fun day! **By the end of this, you're going to feel confident that you can look up any product on Amazon and find gold.**

READY TO ROLL WITH YOUR
NEW "BEST FRIEND"?

Yesterday, we introduced you to the concept of the TSCRK - Top Searched Closest Related Keyword.

Tomorrow, we're going to take it a step further and show you how to find a supplier to manufacture those profitable products. Once the products are ready, you don't have to worry about shipping them yourself. Instead, you can send them directly to Amazon's warehouses. The e-commerce giant will then take care of fulfilling the orders to customers through Prime shipping, and you'll receive payment every two weeks.

This is the Rainmaker Method in a nutshell, and by investing in yourself with this book and still being here on Day 3, you can now consider yourself a Rainmaker!

Our key focus today is where most businesses fail due to the lack of proven demand. Most entrepreneurs struggle to market their products and spend a lot of money on Facebook ads.

However, Amazon has millions of people searching for products every day, which already creates a demand. People don't visit Amazon just to hang out; they visit Amazon to buy what they need!

Let us give you an example. I, Stephen, recently purchased a couch cup holder for our living room. Over time, it started to wear out, and we needed a new one. So, I went on Amazon and searched for the exact item I needed. This is how most people shop on Amazon; they look for precisely what they want and buy from the front page.

However, the front page is not random! Amazon *strategically* places the best-selling items on the front page. **That's why it's crucial to understand how to get on the right aisle and at the right level to be visible**

to buyers. Imagine how many potential customers you could have if your product is visible to thousands of people every month!

With the Rainmaker Method, we are here to help you qualify your product and place it on the right aisle on Amazon. By using Helium 10, we can find search terms and determine what people want to buy on Amazon. Our goal is to help you generate passive income for your family.

So, as we start today, keep in mind that Amazon already has the demand, and with the right product placement and visibility, you can start earning without spending money on offsite ads or social media marketing.

By utilizing proven demand, we're going to make all of our product decisions based on what's already working and selling on Amazon.

Let's start off by going through the three Rainmaker product qualifiers again. By focusing on these qualifiers, you will be able to easily find profitable product ideas that have a proven demand. The three product qualifiers are:

1. Does it sell well?

    Is there a demand?

2. Can you compete?

    We'll show you how to figure that out.

3. Good profit margins?

    You're aiming for a 35 to 55% profit margin, but we won't even run the numbers until we've determined the first two product qualifiers, which is what we will be focusing on today! (This third qualifier is something we will be leaning into, in tomorrow's chapter.)

SOME ADDITIONAL CAVEATS & PITFALLS TO AVOID:

We've learned the following from our personal experiences, and we want to save you from making the same mistakes!

1. **When researching products, focus on those that already sell well.** You don't need to reinvent the wheel or come up with a new invention for Amazon. Instead, use Helium 10 to find out if there's search demand and volume, and I'll show you how to do that.

2. **Find your audience <u>first</u>, then create a product just for them.** You don't want to create a product and then search for the person to buy it. Most businesses make this mistake, and they have to spend a lot on marketing to find those people. By finding the people first and figuring out what they want, you can reduce risk in this process because you're basing what you're launching on data. It's like planting the right plant in the right place! You can't expect to grow tomatoes in the shade... Instead, you need to plant the right plant in the right place. So let's find that **place** first and then put the plant there.

3. **When searching for products, look for ones you can improve and innovate on.** We want to make Amazon a better place to shop. Remember, this is a win-win-win-win! We have to help the customers win. So if you're finding a product, and everyone says it's too small, just make it bigger. Once you find a product, start looking for ways to make Amazon more amazing. Look at the data to figure out

what they want. Ask yourself how you can serve this person who's buying the product. Who are they? How can you offer them more value so that they're thinking, "Oh my goodness, I can pay $18 for this one, or I can buy this one for $18 and get so much more?"

The thing is, you are wired to be creative! Yes, **you**!

Sometimes, we have false beliefs that hold us back. Someone may have said something over us when we were growing up that affected our belief system about ourselves. We want to break that off today, and say that **you are wired to be creative**, even if you're not an artist, painter, or photographer. Even if you're in a science or nursing career, you're still wired to be creative. It's in our human nature! One of our mentors made this point, and we love how he said it. He said that animals can create, like birds that can create nests or beavers that can create dams, but they do the same thing over and over. Humans, on the other hand, have a unique ability to be abundantly creative because it's actually in our nature. **We are creators by nature!**

4. So, if you've ever said, "I'm not creative," we encourage you to cancel that out because it's not true. We believe in the power of words! Cancel out that lie today and say, **"I am wired to be creative! I am a fountain of good ideas!"**

I, Stephen, remember being with some friends who had a two-year-old that kept saying, "I have an idea," but he never shared it with us. It was hilarious because we kept asking him what the idea was, but he would just repeat himself. So I started teaching him to say, "I'm a fountain of good ideas," and it was a great reminder that we constantly have good ideas flowing out of us.

We want you to start saying that to yourself too because today, you're going to get some great ideas. Get ready to be a fountain of good ideas! To get started, try looking at a product on Amazon and ask yourself, "How can I improve that?" This is a great way to start engaging your creativity!

5. Another thing to keep in mind is to **look for evergreen products that consistently sell well.** These are products that are trending in the right direction or are always in demand. We want to play the long game and avoid trends that are here today, gone tomorrow. For example, fidget spinners were a huge trend in 2017, but if you got in on the trend too late, you might have ended up with a lot of inventory you couldn't sell. We'll show you how to identify products that are evergreen or trending in the right direction using data analysis.

6. It's important not to focus solely on "home run" products. While it's possible to make a lot of money on one big hit, these products can be risky and require a lot of effort to maintain. Instead, we recommend **going for base hits** - smaller, consistent products that can add up over time. We'd rather have 10 products selling $10,000 a month than one product selling $100,000 a month. By building up a portfolio of consistent sellers, you can create a more sustainable and passive income stream. Once you've mastered the basics, you

can start breaking the rules and taking bigger risks. But for your first product, it's better to play it safe and go for consistent, sustainable sales.

7. Finally, let's discuss **what to avoid when selling on Amazon**: Some items are restricted, such as weapons and hazardous materials, and it's best to steer clear of those. Additionally, certain products have higher barriers to entry, like topical products or books. While some people flip books on Amazon, it's not the best option for your first product. We also don't recommend selling software, musical instruments, or insurance because these are niche categories with limited trust from customers.

Next, there are some categories to approach with caution. Electronics can be sold, but they require more customer service since Amazon doesn't provide product support.

Cell phone accessories, supplements, beauty consumables, and makeup are also categories to approach with caution. While there is a lot of money to be made in these categories, they are highly competitive, and not everyone plays friendly. We are going after low hanging fruit on Amazon that flies under the radar. We're not calling for big, money-making products, but for base hits that will build up a portfolio over time. This approach will keep your business hands-off and passive!

WORKING FROM REST

Just something we want to remind you of: This is a process, so take your time. We totally get it! We know we have a ton of go-getters, like you may be, who want to hit the ground running. And, we want to applaud you for that. However, if you are feeling overwhelmed and unsure, or starting to feel stuck or things aren't quite clicking, we want to encourage you to take a break!

Go on a walk, spend time with your family, and mentally step away from product research. It can be time-consuming, but we want you to get it right the first time.

We give you permission here to take a break and come back to it if you're feeling like you're hitting a wall. Sometimes, I need a quick 30-minute break when I'm trying to figure something out. I know it's going to click because I see the potential, but I just need that quick break.

Remember, this isn't a hustle! We want to work from a place of rest. If you're feeling exhausted after spending three hours on Helium 10, take a break.

We had a mom in our community who was searching for a product for hours and was feeling exhausted. But after taking a break, her daughter showed her a new toy, which ended up being the product idea she needed! So, don't be afraid to step away and come back refreshed.

Remember, product research is the most important and time-consuming part of this process. But it doesn't always have to involve jumping into the software to make progress on it!

If you feel overwhelmed, take a short break, or try another research method like going shopping. Once you get this down, opportunities are literally everywhere. You'll see potential products and brands everywhere that you can sell.

We're equipping you with the tools to qualify any idea you have, so you know if it's a goldmine on Amazon or something you should put away for later. Just remember that this short season of your time is <u>building the foundation</u> for your business. It should be fun, not over-whelming. And once you really dial in this process, the world will look different. You'll pick up your head and see potential everywhere.

I love this quote by Einstein: "You have to learn the rules of the game, and then you can play better than anyone else." And that's just what we believe. With practice, it will become second nature for you, just like our coaches who can effortlessly spot profitable products and launch them. So keep learning and practicing, and soon you'll be able to qualify any product idea with ease!

THE RAINMAKER FAMILY PRODUCT RESEARCH CHECKLIST

Now, we are about to show you **how to take your first steps in finding the right products to sell on Amazon, using Helium 10!**

We're going to walk you through the Rainmaker family Product Re-search Checklist, which is what we use to qualify ideas.

We'll take it slow, but it's important to note that learning product re-search is like learning a new language - the more you practice, the easier it will become! Some Rainmakers have a breakthrough within a few days, while others take a few weeks. The key is to stick with it and not give up. Remember, you won't have that "clicking" moment if you quit.

THE RAINMAKER FAMILY

Product Research

CHECKLIST

Part 1

Step 1: Start on Helium 10's Magnet tool and search for a keyword related to your product idea.

Step 2: Sort by search volume, high to low.

Step 3: Identify the keywords that are specific to your product. You can verify this by clicking on that keyword to see if those products are related to your product idea (we love keywords that are 5000 searches a month+)

Step 4: Click on the highest searched keyword that is related to your product.

Part 2

Step 5: Start on Amazon and search for that keyword. Open your X-Ray Chrome extension. Check the following:

    a. Are there products with less than 1,000 reviews on the first page?

    b. Is the average price above $15?

    c. Is the average FBA fee less than 50% of the retail price?

    d. Are most products using FBA & are there multiple brands?

    e. Are at least 3 of the top 10 products selling 300+ units per month?

Step 6: If yes to all of the above (Step 5), yay! You've almost qualified your idea.

Step 7: With a quick Alibaba search (see Day 4's training), can you source this product for 4-5 times less than the retail price?

Step 8: Use the Power Profit tool in your Rainmaker app to enter the necessary numbers. If your idea has a profit margin of or above 35-50%, it's time to start reaching out to manufacturers and ordering a sample! You're on your way.

THE Rainmaker FAMILY

Our first step involves using the Helium 10 Magnet Tool to search for a keyword related to the product you want to sell on Amazon. If you're an international seller, you can search in the marketplace where you plan to sell, but most of our Rainmakers sell in the USA because of the larger market size.

Once you've entered your keyword in the search bar, **Step 2 is to sort the results by search volume from high to low**. This should bring up the **Top Searched Closest Related Keyword** (TSCRK) that's most relevant to your product. Look for keywords with search volumes between 4,000 and 25,000 to start.

Now it's time for **Step 3. Go through the list of keywords from the top down and look for the one that matches the closest to what you are selling.**

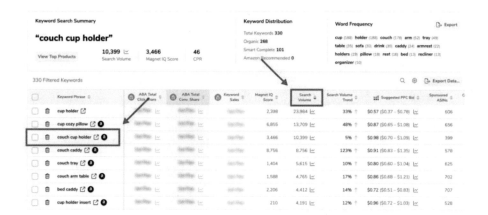

If you're unsure if a keyword fits, click on it to see if it leads you to products that are similar to what you have in mind. If it's not a match, discard it and move on to the next one. Repeat this step until you find the most relevant keyword that has a high search volume. If you can't find it on the first page, move on to the second page and keep going until you find it.

Step 4 is to look at the search results on Amazon for the chosen keyword. Do the products shown match what you have in mind for your product? If they do, great! You've found the right keyword. If not, go back to Step 1 and try a different keyword. Remember, the goal is to find the right "aisle" on Amazon where your product will have high buying intent.

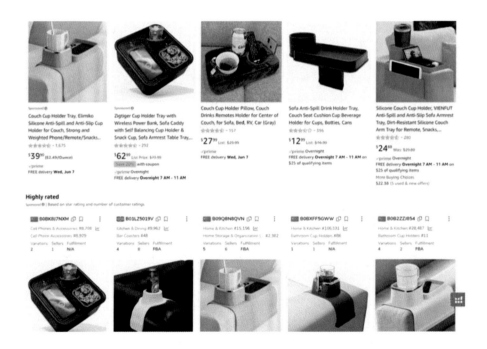

The key is to find high-intention keywords that specifically describe what customers want. For example, if you're selling a couch cup holder, you want to find keywords that are most closely related to this product. Look for keywords that have high search volume and are exactly what customers are looking for.

Step 5 is where we start analyzing the search results on Amazon. This is where we "walk down the aisle" and note if the product is somewhere we can make money. First, you need to open the Helium 10 Chrome Extension, which you should have already installed. Now, click on Xray, which allows you to dig into the behind-the-scenes information about the products on the search results page.

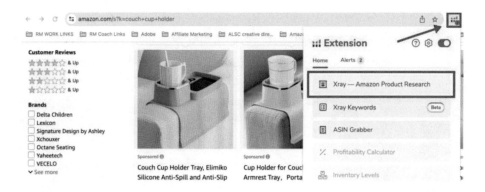

On the Xray page, you will **look for qualifiers that are important for Rainmaker products and base hit products**. For example, you want to make sure the product is not selling millions of units, as that would require a lot of inventory and money. You want to make sure that the product is profitable and reachable for you!

Qualifier 1: Look at the review count, which is an indicator of competition. You can find this column on the right-hand side of the front page listings. Look for products with triple or double-digit reviews, which means that they are relatively new to the market and there is room to compete.

Qualifier 2: Sponsored listings are paid placements, and we want to focus on organic results. If you see sponsored listings, you can skip them or filter them out using the "Hide Sponsored Products" feature.

Qualifier 3: The next factor to consider is the price of the products. Look for an average price over $15 to ensure that the product is profitable after accounting for FBA fees.

Qualifier 4: Check the FBA fees, which are the fees that Amazon charges to store and ship your products, plus 15% of the price of your product (called a referral fee) since they brought the customer to you. Ensure that the fees are low, as high FBA fees could eat into your profits.

Qualifier 5: Look for products that are using FBA as their fulfillment method, as this is the method we recommend using. If all or most of the products on the front page are using a different fulfillment method, such as AMZ or MFN which refers to self-shipping which is not passive, it may be a red flag. You definitely want to see some other people succeeding

with products you want to sell and not take any risks without the data adding up!

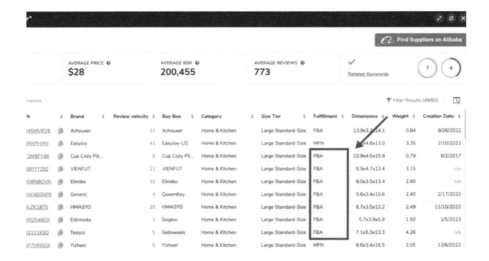

Qualifier 6: Check for multiple brands. We can find this information in the brand column, and it's good to see different brand names on the front page because it indicates an open market. If we see one brand dominating the page, it's probably not worth competing with them.

Lastly, let's consider the quality of the listings. We can do this by looking at the product ratings under the Ratings column. Most of the products have good ratings, but if we see products with lower ratings like threes and fours, it means there's room for improvement and opportunity to create a better product.

Product Details	ASIN	Brand	Ratings	Images	Review velocity	Buy Box	Category	Size Tier
Couch and Bed Cup Holder Pillo...	B0B4SMVXV6	Xchouxer	4.5	5		27 Xchouxer	Home & Kitchen	Large St.
Couch Cup Holder, Easyjoy Silico...	B0BRKPHJNY	Easyjoy	4.1	8		41 Easyjoy-US	Home & Kitchen	Large St.
Cup Cozy Pillow (Gray) *As Seen ...	B072M9FV46	Cup Cozy Pill...	4.7	8		6 Cup Cozy Pil...	Home & Kitchen	Large St.
Silicone Couch Cup Holder, VIEN...	B0B8RYYZBZ	VIENFUT	4.3	9		21 VIENFUT	Home & Kitchen	Large St.
Couch Cup Holder Tray, Elimiko Si...	B09O8NBOVN	Elimiko	4.5	9		32 Elimiko	Home & Kitchen	Large St.
QueenKey Couch Cup Holder, Sil...	B0BW4BSNP6	Generic	4.4	7		4 QueenKey	Home & Kitchen	Large St.
HMASYO Couch Cup Holder Tray...	B0BLZK18T5	HMASYO	4.5	8		20 HMASYO	Home & Kitchen	Large St.
Cup Holder for Couch	The Ultim...	B0BRO546DX	Edinnoda	4.0	7		3 Gogloo	Home & Kitchen	Large St.
Tessco 2 Pack Couch Cup Holder ...	B0B2111KSO	Tessco	4.3	6		5 Getoweals	Home & Kitchen	Large St.

Let's practice with this product specifically. Once you begin, your creativity will flow. You can even involve your kids or family members, like these Rainmakers who played the creativity game in the car. They would come up with a product, like a coaster for your table, and then everyone would brainstorm ideas on how to make it better and serve the person on a higher level.

Now, let's apply this to the armrest cup holder. You might not be an expert in armrest cup holders, but you probably sit on the couch and use a cup. When we bought this product, we chose one with hinges on the sides. Over time, as we put drinks on it, it messed up our couch by leaving marks. So, we got a silicone one that was softer and wouldn't leave impressions on the couch.

What can we do to make this armrest cup holder better? Here are a couple of really creative ideas we've heard! Some suggestions include: adding a charging port, offering a trendy design, making it dishwasher safe, making it attachable so toddlers can't throw it, making it more modern, creating different colors for different couches, adding a pocket on the side, making it wipeable or machine washable if it's fabric, making it waterproof on the outside with cushioning on the bottom, or making the cup holder expandable to fit different cup sizes.

One seller was even smarter and added a little insert that you could pull out of the cup holder to put a coffee mug in with the handle. Genius, right? Serious sellers ask themselves, "How can we improve? How can we make it better?"

We're only five steps into the checklist, and you're doing great! Let's keep going. This product is looking promising so far, and there are ways we can still improve it.

One way is to look at all the negative reviews. Find someone with a lot of reviews and some negative ones. For example, a product with 900 reviews and 4 stars means there must be some negative reviews. Click on that product and then click on the Helium 10 Chrome Extension. Go to "Review Insights."

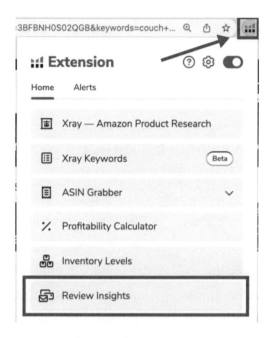

Use the filter to see only the one-star and two-star reviews. By reading these reviews, we can learn about the customers and what they want.

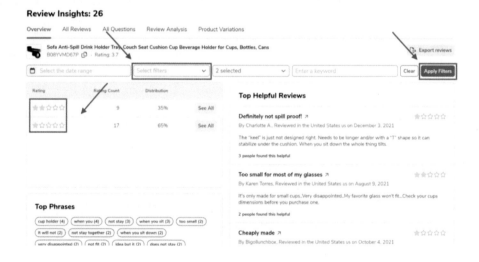

For example, one review says that the cup holder doesn't stay in place and slides off the arm of the chair. Another review says it's too small and flimsy. These are valuable insights that can help us improve the product and serve the customer at a higher level. By taking the data and negative reviews into account, we can be creative and find ways to make the product better.

Just one thing to note from Rainmakers we've seen: When coming up with ideas, it's important to avoid falling into the trap of creating something because you think it's a good idea. Instead, **make sure your decisions are based on data**. Don't just assume that a zebra print will be popular because you like zebras. Look at what people are actually saying and what data is telling you. If you see that there is demand for a zebra print in the reviews, then you can consider it. But always make sure that you have evidence to back up your ideas. If you can provide data from sources like Pinterest, Tik-Tok, or Google Trends, then it's worth considering and testing. We don't take risks without proof, so make sure your ideas are grounded in data!

Now, we're going to keep using Xray to avoid looking at the wrong keywords and data. **One way to spot if you're on the wrong track is to follow Step 6.** The search volume you are looking for needs to be between 4,000-25,000, with evergreen sales that match up with the search volume. If sales are too high and search volume is low, you're likely looking at the wrong keyword.

In Steps 7 and 8, we'll examine the numbers on the Power Profit Tool. We're aiming for profit margins between 35% and 55% or higher.

You can access the Rainmaker Web App at
www.rainmakerchallenges.com/bookresources
to get help with product research.

Inside the app, we have provided you with the basic version of the Power Profit Tool, while our mastermind members have access to the fully unlocked version that helps with planning various things. However, for now, all you need is the basic version as you are just conducting product research to determine if a product will work.

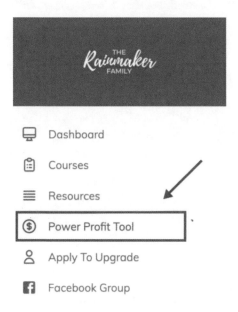

So, you will have two tabs open - **the Product Qualifier Tool** and **the potential product you are examining**. With Helium 10, we will soon also show you how to talk to a manufacturer to determine the cost of producing the product with the desired improvements. For now, we want to determine if the product fits within our budget and profit margins at a quick glance. Here, let us show you a useful hack:

We will find a product similar to the one we want to sell, and on the specific listing, click on Helium 10 and then select the profitability calculator. Don't be intimidated by the various numbers; **focus on the unit**

manufacturing cost, which is the most important number. Typically, people source products that cost around $2 to $5, but this product's unit manufacturing cost is a little higher, which explains the higher price point.

Let's enter this product into the Power Profit Tool, starting by entering the product details, such as the title and description, and taking note of any areas for improvement. Keep in mind that most manufacturers have a minimum order quantity, which typically ranges from 250 to 1000 units. For this example, let's use 250 as our minimum, and the cost per unit is $7.08, but let's round it up to $8.

Now, let's take a look at the FBA fees for this product on Amazon. We recommend checking the fees for similar products to get a better idea of the average cost, considering that you may change the size or price of the product. Since this is a higher-priced product, some listings are making up to $19,000/month, which is impressive. Based on the fees we've seen, we estimate that the FBA fees for this style will be around $10-$11.

When conducting product research, it's a good idea to round up the figures to ensure you're within the 35% to 55% profit margin. Keep in mind that Amazon retail for this product is around $38. Shipping costs can be tricky, but we can get a rough estimate from the Profitability Calculator. The unit freight cost for this product is $2.78, which is a good average to work with. By multiplying this with the number of units, we get an estimate of $700.

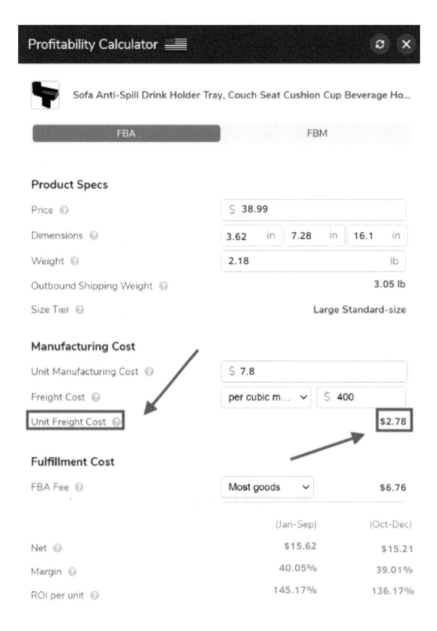

Now, we can add all the numbers to the Power Profit Tool and evaluate the metrics. The profit margin is 42%, which is within the desired range of 35% to 55%. The total cost of manufacturing and shipping the product is $2,700, and the projected profit is $4,000, which is above our target.

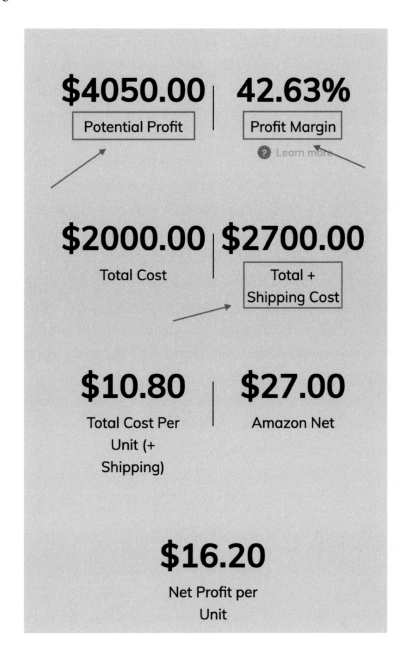

You can make a profit of $6,000 to $7,000 depending on the sales volume. When scaling up to 500 or 1000 units, you can see how profitable it can be. Most sellers are selling hundreds of units each month, with some making up to $19,000.

In summary, Step 8 on our checklist is to determine if the product fits on Amazon and whether the numbers look promising. Remember, we're not investing in the product yet, just evaluating its potential and if the numbers look good.

If you're feeling good about the product so far, it's time to go back to **Step 7**: **Connect with a manufacturer to get accurate pricing for the product,** which we'll cover in detail tomorrow. We'll provide you with scripts to use that make the process super easy without the need for phone calls.

It's important to note that the price provided by Helium 10 is just an estimate and may not be entirely accurate. In reality, you may end up paying less, such as $4 or $5 per unit for the product. This is why it's crucial to communicate directly with the manufacturer to obtain the actual costs.

After you've spoken with a manufacturer and obtained accurate numbers, input them again into the Power Profit Tool. Now's the time to plug in the actual costs, including shipping and the cost per unit to double-check everything. This ensures that we have the most up-to-date and accurate information before moving forward.

Tomorrow, we'll teach you the remaining steps, including how to talk to the manufacturer and reduce risk by ordering a sample of the product before committing to a larger order.

Congratulations! You've completed your "workout" for today - going through your Rainmaker Family's Product Research Checklist. We are so proud of you!

Take a deep breath and a refreshing drink, and we'll see you tomorrow!

YOUR DAY 3
QUICK WIN:

PRACTICE USING HELIUM 10 TODAY!

Action-takers are money-makers! Are you ready to take action and set yourself up for success?

Your Quick Win today is to practice using Helium 10, following along with your Rainmaker Family Product Research Checklist.

You'll find this at
www.rainmakerchallenges.com/bookresources
along with a valuable bonus training and additional resources designed to enhance your experience as you journey through this book.

Make a post in our Rainmaker Family Facebook group with **#familyfreedombook** to let us know how you went. We'd love to cheer you on!

Rainmaker Family Challenge!

DAY THREE

Finding Gold & Our Step By Step Repeatable Process

Today you are going to learn how to easily sift through Amazon and find a **"gold mine"** of products that anyone can launch with the right tools and knowledge.

Today's Action Step:

Step One	Step Two
Watch **Finding Gold** Training	Practice Using **Helium 10**

Are you ready? Let's get started!

Rainmaker

#CELEBRATIONS

Rainmaker Saralynn:

"I am a homeschooling stay-at-home mom to two wonderful boys. My husband and I toyed with the idea of me going back to school for a particular degree because we needed some help with our financial situation. One day I was standing in my kitchen re-heating a cup of tea for probably the fifteenth time because, mom life, and I saw the Rainmaker ad. Something in me whispered, 'You should click this link and take this challenge.' I instantly knew that I found my people when I started the challenge. And then day three came I was like, 'oh my gosh, what is Helium 10?'

I found my new passion and it was so fun. When the kid and I would go out to the store we all would be curious what the numbers were for that particular item and get excited to look it up when we got home. I loved that I was getting even my kids excited and teaching them how to be entrepreneurs. Everything in our life now is, 'I wonder what the numbers are.'

Rainmakers has been life changing. I love getting the biweekly checks from Amazon, of course. But for me, mostly it's the power of change that I've made in myself. Believing in myself more and I feel like I'm no longer dreaming with my eyes closed. I'm dreaming with my eyes open because I'm living the dream that I've always wanted."

8

DAY FOUR:
IDEA TO REALITY

Today we're going to teach you how to transform a product idea into physical reality!

In this chapter, we'll guide you through the process step by step. This experience will change your life forever, as you'll be able to build an entire business model based on the secrets we'll be sharing here with you.

Today marks a turning point because after today, you'll be able to say, "I have connections."

Our personal story on how we created our first product began in the wedding world. We were highly skilled at creating wedding videos and photos which led to potential clients approaching us for media projects. They wanted videos for local businesses, products, and more.

This led us to the niche of Kickstarter. We set up a website called "Kickstarter Got Video", where people sent us their products and we created videos for them! We watched these products succeed on Kickstarter, generating millions of dollars. This sparked our curiosity. How were these people creating products?

During that time I, Stephen, became obsessed with the idea of product creation. I initially believed it involved a lengthy process, including prototypes, designers, CAD models, and patenting.

However, as I delved deeper into the subject, I realized I had many misconceptions about the difficulty of making a product. One year, we set a goal to figure it all out. We compiled a list of product ideas and aimed to learn the ins and outs of product creation.

At the time, I became interested in a niche hobby: kendama. Kendamas are Japanese wooden toys, featuring a ball and cups used to catch the ball. Chelsey got a kendama for me for Christmas, and though it may seem odd, I grew addicted to it.

I thought, "This could be the product we take a risk on." Despite being a small niche, its community was passionate and eager for new products. We embarked on a journey to learn how to manufacture a product, starting with a kendama accessory.

Our first product was a small putty accessory for kendamas. Known as tungsten putty, it's used in fishing for its weight. Kendama enthusiasts prefer their toys to have a specific weight, which led us to try selling this product.

Unfamiliar with Amazon, we ordered the product for about $1 per unit. We got a quote from a manufacturer and it was $500 for the order. It was terrifying, as at the time, that was a lot of money for us! I thought, "I hope we're not getting scammed. Chelsey's going to kill me if I send money to some scam artist on the internet thinking I'm going to buy a bunch of products."

Yet when the box arrived, we knew we had created something. I said to Chelsey, "We made a product!" I literally sat there and stuck stickers on by hand for every unit, all 500 of them.

We went on to sell these items for about $9.99 each, mostly on Instagram. It was our first taste of e-commerce, and I thought, "Wow, we did this thing!" We learned a great deal from this experience and it proved to us that we could bring a product idea to life.

SHATTERING LIMITING BELIEF SYSTEMS

There's an old saying that goes "You can't judge a book by its cover." It's a wise adage that reminds us not to make assumptions based on surface-level information. I was reminded of this truth recently when I had a conversation with a friend about pit bulls. Growing up, I had a few bad experiences with pit bulls, and I'll admit, I was afraid of them. But then I met Lars, a pit bull that belonged to some of our friends. This was the sweetest dog ever!

Even a couple of years ago, when we brought our son Kaizen over to our good friends' house, Lars the pitbull was playing with him and was so gentle!

Lars shattered all the negative stereotypes I had about pit bulls. It made me realize that I had been judging these dogs based on false beliefs and preconceived notions. It was a powerful lesson that taught me to keep an open mind and not judge things based on superficial information.

That's a lesson that applies to so many areas of life, including manufacturing. If you want to make a wood product, you need to go to the place in the world where that product is made best. The same goes for plastic products or any other type of item. It's like planning a wedding. You wouldn't ask a photographer to play music, right? You go to the experts in each area to ensure you get the best possible result.

Unfortunately, there are a lot of misconceptions out there about manufacturing. Some people believe that the only place to make products is in the USA. But the truth is that most things are made all over the world, and not all things made in the USA are actually made in the USA. The Ford F150, which is often considered the quintessential American car, is only about 55% made in the USA and Canada. Meanwhile, the Honda Accord is made with about 65% USA and Canadian It just goes to show that we can't always trust the assumptions we make.

China is currently the leader in manufacturing, and while some people might have negative associations with that fact, the reality is that China has advanced significantly in recent years. They have machinery, robotics, and other tools that make the manufacturing process much more efficient. Of course, there are cultural differences to consider when working with manufacturers in other countries, but that's just a reality of doing business in our globalized world.

During one of our weekly coffee outings, we ran into someone who had participated in the Rainmaker Challenge. Although we didn't know her, she expressed her gratitude for the positive and beautiful way we described China and its people. She had lived in China for almost seven years and fell in love with the country and its people. She thanked us for sharing the amazing culture and positive aspects of the country. It was heartwarming to hear her appreciation!

When it comes to working with Chinese manufacturers, it's important to remember that there are good and bad people in every country. We shouldn't label everyone based on negative stereotypes. For instance, Tina, who we know personally, has been working for six years, an hour away from her kids, to serve Americans. She is just one example of a Chinese citizen who is dedicated to serving others.

We've had the opportunity to connect with many people like Tina and Leo, who own a small manufacturing company that produces kendama products. They are proud of their craft, and we've developed a strong relationship with them.

As we work with Chinese manufacturers, we need to understand the cultural differences that exist in an honor-based society like China. For instance, they don't want to say no to you, which means that they may cut corners to meet your price requirements. This can lead to products that aren't of the best quality, which is why we emphasize the importance of sample inspections and having checkpoints in the manufacturing process.

This is why we teach our Rainmakers negotiation keys so that you can strike a balance between getting what you need in terms of profit margins while ensuring that the quality of your products isn't compromised.

OUR "IDEAS TO REALITY" 7-STEP CHECKLIST

What would it be like for you if you could confidently source high-quality products from manufacturers all over the world?

Imagine having the ability to connect with suppliers who are affordable, ethical, and people you'd be proud to work with. Think about the sense of pride you'd feel knowing that you're supporting these businesses and building relationships that could last for years to come.

As with any industry, there are good and bad "eggs". In today's chapter, we're going to show you how to find a good supplier!

Let's start by pulling up **your Rainmakers Web App**. Go to **Resources** and then click on **Sourcing and Manufacturing**. There, you'll find a variety of resources for sourcing products all over the world.

Alibaba is one of the main sourcing websites that many Rainmakers use. While it's not the only platform out there, it is definitely the leader in terms of connecting with manufacturers.

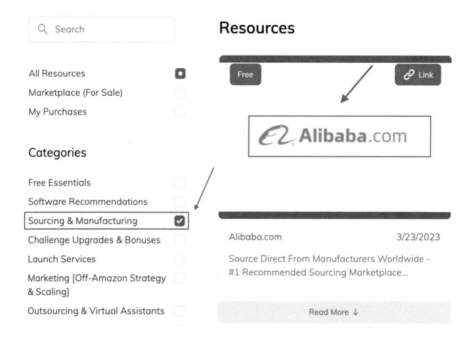

Think of it as the Amazon of manufacturing.

Anyone can create a free account on Alibaba, so why don't you go ahead and create yours now!

After creating an account, you can start communicating with manufacturers. It will ask for a business name, but don't worry about it too much, as you can edit it later before actually ordering products.

Remember, you should not move on to the manufacturing phase until you've qualified your product! This ensures you don't waste the manufacturer's time and are fully prepared for the sourcing process.

Let's go over our 7-Step Sourcing Checklist to help you get started:

THE RAINMAKER FAMILY

7 Step Sourcing
CHECKLIST

Learning to connect, negotiate, and produce quality products is a
powerful skill you are about to learn!

☐ Identify a profitable product opportunity using the Rainmaker Product Research Checklist
(See Day 3's Training in The Rainmaker Challenge).

☐ Navigate to Alibaba.com - Our recommended starting place for connecting with
manufacturers.

☐ Use the search bar to search for your idea.

☐ Click on "Verified manufacturers".

☐ Check the two boxes on the left hand side: "Trade Assurance" and "Verified Supplier"
which will keep you safe, secure, and working with the highest quality manufacturers.

☐ Now, scroll down & click on "Company profile" and look for these things:

- Number of years in business: 3+
- Business type: Manufacturer or Trading Company OR just Manufacturer
- Company Certifications: ISO9001 (Quality Certification). Not required but a bonus!
- Product Density: Does this manufacturer specialize in making the main material in your product?

Notice how these
are all in the same
niche/material.

☐ Message 3-5 suppliers using our Sourcing Script (customize to fit your product!) found on the
next page and input the numbers on the Power Profit Tool found on the Rainmaker Web App.

*Continue the conversation to customize the product to your specifications and then order a
sample to check quality. Once you have a quality sample you'd be proud to sell, bulk order
your product using Trade Assurance!*

THE
Rainmaker
FAMILY

Step 1 is to **identify a probable product opportunity using your Product Research Checklist**. (Hint: We taught you how to do this on Day 3!)

Step 2 is to **navigate to Alibaba.com**, our recommended starting place for connecting with manufacturers.

Step 3 is to **use the search bar to search for your idea**.

Step 4 is to **click on "All Suppliers"**.

Step 5 is to **check the 2 boxes on the left side of the screen: "Verified Manufacturers" and "Trade Assurance"**.

Verified manufacturers have gone through a lot of checkpoints, and working with them will weed out a lot of headaches. Trade assurance is a program that Alibaba has, similar to eBay's PayPal protection program. If something goes wrong with your product, trade assurance has your back. Always work with manufacturers that have this program and are verified.

Now that you've sorted your search by verified manufacturers and trade assurance, start scrolling down, looking for potential manufacturers that could make the product you want to sell.

To make sure you're dealing with legit manufacturers, you'll need to qualify them by checking out their information. For example, at the time of this writing, I'm looking at this manufacturer called Dongguan, which has been in business for 12 years, has 50 staff members, and does about 50,000 transactions a year (give or take). I can even visit their profile to look around their office and warehouse.

However, before you message anyone, there are a few things you'll want to check to ensure you're qualifying a solid manufacturer. Here they are:

First, you'll need to check if they're a manufacturer or a trading company. It's important to go directly to the manufacturer, because working with a middleman will usually result in a higher price point. So, you want to ensure it says "manufacturer" under their company profile.

Next, you can look at product certification. Different manufacturers can get certified for different things, and we prefer ISO 9000, which is a quality certification. It's not necessary, but it's a bonus if they have it. You can see if a manufacturer has ISO 9000 or other certifications by checking their profile.

One of the biggest game changers we've discovered in recent years is product density. When you look at a manufacturer's products, you want to see if they're selling a lot of the same type of thing or same material. For example, if you're planning to make your product out of silicone, you want to see if a manufacturer specializes in silicone. We can tell this by checking their product density, which means they're selling a lot of the same thing. This is good because it means they have the most specialized machinery and robotics for that material and can offer us the lowest cost. We can hover over their products list and see if they specialize in what we need.

You'll also want to look at their photos, check if they have 5 out of 5 satisfied reviews, and respond quickly within four hours.

Once you've identified three to five promising manufacturers using the sourcing criteria we discussed earlier, **it's time to contact them in Step 6.**

Alibaba offers a convenient "Contact Supplier" button on their platform. Simply use our customizable Sourcing Script here to guide your conversation with these manufacturers!

SOURCING SCRIPT

Hello,

My name is **YOUR NAME** and I am from **BUSINESS NAME**. I am interested in placing an order for **INSERT PRODUCT NAME/LINK**. I just have a few questions beforehand:

What is your minimum order quantity?

What is your cost per unit at the minimum order as well as if I were to order 3x your minimum order?

What are your payment terms for new customers?

I would also like to order a sample of **PRODUCT** to verify quality. Can you please send me the cost for the sample? Please include shipping to:

YOUR ADDRESS

Thank you,

YOUR NAME

Don't worry if this script seems complicated at first. It's designed to get essential information like minimum order quantity, cost per unit, and payment terms. We even ask a somewhat confusing question on purpose to test their English proficiency and ensure effective communication.

Understanding these details will help you know if the manufacturer's offer is within your budget and if there are opportunities to negotiate pricing with larger orders. You can also plug these numbers into your Power Profit Tool to evaluate the potential profit margin.

When messaging suppliers, don't hesitate to make customizations or request improvements to the product. This is your opportunity to improve on the product and make it something you're proud to sell!

Once you've narrowed down your list, Step 7 is to **order a sample and ensure it meets your standards for quality**. Remember, it's not just about getting products on Amazon. Your success depends on offering good products that meet your customers' demands.

After you have talked to manufacturers and selected the right one, it's important to remember to **update your product checklist and profit margins with the real numbers you receive**. Before you invest more time and resources in innovating and customizing the product, always double-check the financial viability of the project for yourself, your family, and your business.

And as soon as you have a quality sample you'd be proud to sell, you're now ready to **bulk order your product using Trade Assurance**. This is the final step in the manufacturing process. Congratulations on learning how to turn your ideas into a reality by finding a profitable product!

READY TO COMPRESS TIME?
HERE'S A BONUS RESOURCE!

We're going to show you something that can help you save time in the next 2 minutes.

Let's go back to the Rainmaker App and navigate to the "Sourcing" tab under "Resources." Here, you'll find options like Thompson Maker's Row, which is based in the USA. While we've worked with them before, we ultimately found that they weren't a good fit for us. Instead, we sourced about half of our products through Alibaba, and the other half through a sourcing agent called Jing Sourcing.

You may be asking, "What is a sourcing agent, Stephen and Chelsey?" Well, a sourcing agent acts as a middleman between you and the manufacturer.

If you have more time on your hands and want to have more ownership over your product, then going through Alibaba and building those relationships with manufacturers is a great option. However, if you're short on time, we would recommend going through a sourcing agent. While they will charge you 5-10% of your order, they have a network of over 2,000 manufacturers that they work with, which means they can get you better prices and can handle everything from customizing products to shipping and handling.

Jing Sourcing, for example, can handle all of your needs, and you'll only pay the 5-10% fee when you place your order. They can even offer free product photography, quality inspection, and warehousing for up to two months if you need it. It's a great resource for those who are looking to save time and get the best possible prices!

Click here to check them out:
www.rainmakerchallenges.com/jing

We wanted to share this with you because we know some of you are in the Stuck Mama or Hustle Mama phase where time is of the essence. If so, this is the way to do it.

Our goal is to empower you with these resources so that you can create products at a fraction of the cost and achieve success in your business!

Speaking of resources, let us show you what's in our 12-month Rainmaker Mastermind Coaching Program. It will help you continue to keep the momentum going past our seven days here together towards seeing the full extent of the results that our community is known for.

WHAT YOUR FUTURE COULD BE LIKE...

What would it be like for you to be a part of a community that celebrates your wins regularly, and helps you create a business you love that generates a monthly income of $10k to $30k with the potential for a seven-figure exit?

Our approach is entirely remote, which means you can work from anywhere in the world and enjoy the benefits of being your own boss. Imagine being freed to travel with your family while still earning a reliable income, without worrying about being tied down to a physical location!

Our mastermind provides the best classroom learning, not just from us, but also from a community of six and seven-figure Rainmaker families. You'll have access to resources and strategies that have been tested and proven to work in the Amazon FBA space.

Imagine having a skill set that's recession-proof and valuable in the marketplace... With our program, you'll be equipped with the tools and knowledge to succeed in the Amazon FBA space, whether you want to sell your products or help other companies grow their sales.

Our goal is for you to have the financial confidence to never worry about money again. What would it be like for you to enjoy the peace of mind that comes with knowing that you have a steady income stream that you can rely on?

With Amazon FBA, you won't have to rent a physical storefront, learn how to be a salesperson, build complex funnels or websites, run Facebook or Instagram ads, invest in risky real estate, join an MLM, or promote someone else's product for slim returns.

Imagine the freedom that comes with knowing that you can achieve financial freedom on your terms with the easiest way to create leverage for your family!

So here's what's included in our program:

- We offer seven weekly coaching clinics that are available to you every single week and are there for you whenever you need them.

- On Tuesdays, we have two Product Powerup sessions you can join anytime you have questions.

- Once you find your product, you can join our launch and sourcing experts who will help you with manufacturing and guide you through the process.

- Then, after launch, you will optimize your product. For the first two months of the program, you will have a personalized coach to hold your hand, answer any questions you have, and offer guidance on your product selection. This person will also hold you accountable, a significant reason why most people fail. They lack accountability!

- In addition to coaching, you will receive a 60-minute business consultation and 24/7 email support.

- We bring in tons of highly-experienced guest trainers and teachers while offering additional resources and tools.

- For example, we have the advanced version of the Power Profit Tool that you've experienced in the basic version so far. Additionally, we have the Move the Needle Tool that helps you step-by-step through the entire process. We also have an 11-Point Checklist that you can use to evaluate every product and determine if it's a good fit for your business.

- We're currently on Day Four of our seven-day journey here, and we want to encourage you to keep going with us. That's why we're giving you a sneak peek overview of all the additional goodness in store for you inside of our Mastermind opportunity to get you excited!

Completing this 7-day jumpstart is no small feat, and we're proud of you for making it this far. It takes a certain type of person to succeed in this program, and since you are still here with us on Day 4. We're confident that if you stick with us, you'll achieve the results you desire!

YOUR DAY 4

QUICK WIN:

TAKE YOUR PRODUCT IDEA THROUGH OUR 7-STEP "IDEAS TO REALITY" SOURCING CHECKLIST TODAY!

Are you ready to turn your product ideas into reality and start making money? The key to success is taking action, and we're here to help you do just that.

Today's Quick Win is to **take one of your product ideas through our 7-Step "Ideas to Reality" Sourcing Checklist**.

Once you've gone through the checklist, we want to hear from you! Make a post in our Rainmaker Family Facebook group with #familyfreedombook to let us know how it went. Our community is here to support and cheer you on every step of the way.

Remember, action-takers are money-makers. Don't let your ideas stay just ideas – turn them into a reality and start your journey towards financial freedom!!

Rainmaker Family Challenge!

DAY FOUR
Idea to Reality

Today's training will change your life forever and you could build an **entire business model** on what you are about to learn how to go from product idea to **physical reality.**

Today's Action Steps:

☐ Step One	☐ Step Two
Read **Day Four's** training	**Go Live** In The FB Group And Tell Us How Your Life Would Be Different In 12 Months If This Idea To Reality Took Place

Are you ready? Let's get started!

Rainmaker

#CELEBRATIONS

Rainmaker Emily:

"Before Rainmakers, I was working part-time in a stressful job, and I really wanted to be able to stay home with my kids and eventually homeschool when my kids got older. Before Rainmakers, I didn't know anything about selling on Amazon or FBA. Being a few years into my business, I'm now able to be home with my kids, and I'm able to homeschool my oldest this fall.

I am so excited to be able to say that I'm paying myself the same salary that I used to make working part-time, and we're growing little by little. I don't have a lot of time to invest into my business, *but the time that I am able to give is stretched by using the methods that Stephen and Chelsey teach in Rainmakers.*

So, with the little bit of time that I have and the little bit of money that I was able to put in, I've seen that money and time multiply in my life for my family, and we're seeing our financial future change forever."

9

DAY FIVE: SIX-FIGURE ROADMAP

What would it be like for you if you stopped focusing on the *negative* "what ifs" and started imagining the *positive* ones?

What if you could serve a group of people that have never been served before, make a difference in the world, and leave a legacy of financial stability for your family?

These are the possibilities that lie ahead... but only if you choose to believe in them.

Instead of being defined by your past experiences or failures, you can choose to believe that the sky's the limit and anything is possible. Your words have the power to create worlds, and with hard work and the support of our community, we believe that you too, can achieve amazing things.

Imagine what your life could be like a year from now if you start leading with positivity. Could you be one of our big success stories walking across the stage, sharing your success with this group on your Rainmaker anniversary? Could you be taking more vacations with your family or retiring your husband?

What are the things that are in your heart but have felt out of reach due to lack of time or money that would become possible for you?

Today, we are going to talk about creating a Six-Figure Roadmap for you and your family. We call this "Rainmaker Time" because we compress decades into days here!

However, just one word of caution before we go any further. We've packed a lot into this week, but **if you're not taking action, you won't see results.**

Think of it like planting a seed – you can't just plant it and expect it to grow without nurturing it! Similarly, you need to take action and execute the knowledge we've shared with you to see results.

Over the past five days, we've gone deep into some important topics:

On Day 1, we discussed leveraging your time and income to create more for your family. We showed you how Amazon FBA can unlock the potential for a scalable business without burning out.

Day 2 was all about money – we addressed common myths about limited resources and showed you how to start this business with minimal investment. We also shared how Helium 10 can save you time and money when launching profitable products.

On Day 3, we talked about finding gold by going through our Product Research Checklist to ensure you make no risky moves in your business.

And on Day 4, we taught you how to take your ideas and turn them into reality, with expert secrets that can make you a pro sourcing agent.

Today, on Day 5, we're going to give you the fast path to wealth - your Six-Figure Roadmap. We'll show you how to compress your time and achieve financial success – faster!

Do you ever feel like you're taking action but not seeing results? Here's what you can do right now to make sure you stay on track: Keep taking action, but make sure it's effective action.

We talked a lot about taking action this week, but there's something even better than just taking action, and that's **taking effective action**. We see a lot of early-stage entrepreneurs get excited and take action, but often they're working on the wrong things. For example, getting business cards won't necessarily move your business forward!

That's why we often ask ourselves a simple question: **What can I do today to move the needle towards my goal?**

If your goal is to get to $10,000 a month, how do you move the needle towards that goal every single day? **It's about taking small steps that add up over time, rather than focusing on future problems that may never even arise.**

Remember, today has enough worries of its own. Don't worry about tomorrow just yet. Focus on the present moment and take effective action towards your goal every day. This will help you avoid getting stuck in the unknown and keep you in momentum.

We've given you a lot of information this week, and it's up to you to take action and make it count. And if you have been a "passive reader", now is the time for you to step up and take effective action! **You can do this! We believe in you.**

And, if you have been keeping up with the challenge, congratulations! You're part of the 1% who make it all the way to day five. These seven days are a great qualifier to make sure this business is a good fit for you before you invest in a program to help you go further & faster with it. **If you're here with us on Day 5, we know that you have the time, mindset, and commitment to make it happen.**

So keep taking effective action towards your goals and focus on what you can do <u>today</u>. Don't let future problems hold you back. Let's go!

EVALUATING YOUR PROGRESS

Do you remember the story of our first conference experience? That one session we invested in saved us so much time and gave us the freedom we needed. We were left wondering why we hadn't done it before... If you're here investing in yourself for the first time, we're glad you took this step because it's worth it!

Let's dive into the Lifestyle Freedom Model we talked about earlier in the challenge. We discussed the three types of mamas that could be joining us: the Hustle Mama, the Stuck Mama, and the Boxed Mama.

Take a look at your chart if you filled it out earlier this week. Has your dot moved over the last few days?

Do you remember that we shared that this isn't a get-rich-quick scheme? While we've had many families cross the six-figure mark, it won't happen in just seven days. This book is merely the seed we're planting to take you there.

However, the journey to becoming a Rainmaker Mama with complete time and financial freedom is no walk in the park. There will be ups and downs, distractions, and things that will want to throw you off track.

Remember the Seven Levels Deep exercise you did on Day 1? It's important to come back to why you want this and what's important to you. If you find yourself losing momentum, go back and remind yourself of why you're doing this in the first place.

Let me, Chelsey, share a moment we had when I once had a flat tire. It threw off our day and made me think about what some of our mamas might be feeling right now.

Maybe you felt pushback this week, or things came up like fear or past trauma, or fear of the unknown. Maybe your kids got sick or life circumstances got in the way. When we're fighting for something that feels like a true breakthrough, it can seem like there's a wall that we have to actually *break* through!

A friend reminded me that **to get to that breakthrough, we have to break through something**. That could mean learning new things or investing in ourselves, even if it's uncomfortable. But are you willing to break through that barrier? Remember, it's worth it!

BECOMING THE PERSON YOU NEED TO BE... TO LIVE THE LIFE YOU WANT TO LIVE

Let's talk about the most important question you need to ask yourself: **Who do you need to become to achieve your goals**? That's the real question.

We've talked about what you want and why you want it, but as Einstein said, the same thinking that got you here won't get you there. You need to shift your mindset and your identity. Start thinking like a Rainmaker! (If you're not a mom, that's okay too. You can still be a Rainmaker.)

What would a Rainmaker do? They wouldn't say, "Maybe I'll get fit first before joining the gym," or "Maybe I'll make some money first before investing in a program." They'd take action because they believe in themselves.

The key to success is leverage, and that's what Amazon gives us. With their trust and traffic, you don't have to worry about driving traffic yourself or marketing to friends and family. You just plug into their system and get paid to help Amazon win customers and manufacturers win sales. A true win-win for everyone!

If you've tried a business in the past and it didn't work out, it's not your fault. Most businesses fail for many reasons, but Amazon truly solves all those problems. They have proven demand and trust. All we have to do is make educated decisions based on data and serve the people. That's how we do this business.

The cool thing with Amazon is you can scale this business as fast as you have money or faith. If you're starting with little or nothing, we'll show you ways to start with nothing. And if you have some investment to go towards this, you can scale very fast. Money can be scary, but it's just a tool. We'll talk about creative ways to leverage financing and funding for your business in tomorrow's funding clinic.

If you feel like you're not starting with anything, are you willing to borrow an apple to grow an apple tree? Borrowing money to build a money factory is an **investment**, not a liability.

Money can amplify what's in your heart, and help you achieve your goals. And that's what this challenge is all about - helping you achieve your goals and become the person you need to be to get there.

YOUR SIX-FIGURE ROADMAP

Let's talk about the Six-Figure Roadmap because a lot of you are probably wondering "Stephen & Chelsey, this all sounds great... but how can I actually make six figures with this business?"

It's much simpler than you might think! On average, most Rainmaker products that meet the search volume qualifiers we've provided make between $3,000 and $10,000 per month per product. That's a great number to have in your head because it helps you plan your financial future.

All it takes is three products on Amazon using this Rainmaker Method to hit $100,000 in a year. This is your next 12 months we're talking about. Conservatively, three products will definitely get you there, but if you want to aim higher, you may need to create more. This is how you do it.

Now, picture this as a seed. This is your financial life for the next 12 months. You're going to start by investing in your business and buying your inventory for the first time. It's scary, but you have to take that first step of faith and plant the seed. You might feel scared and uncertain, wondering if it will fail, but you have to shift your mindset to the positive. **Instead of worrying about the what-ifs, focus on what could happen if you succeed.** When you launch your product on Amazon, you'll increase your income and reach a new level.

Then, it's time to take another step of faith. You'll need to reorder your inventory before you run out and invest in a second product. Once you launch your second product, you'll be at a new level again.

This is how we level up Rainmakers over 12 months. They go from their default family income to a new normal. You build up a resistance level so even if you retire a product, your income won't drop back down to where it used to be.

The key to this shift is to stop treating more money as your goal. Money is just a tool to help you reach your "why." Your "why" is what's important, such as creating family memories and providing for your family. It's more important than the finances in your bank account. We recommend pursuing vision, not provision. Make money work for you, instead of working for money. Say this with us: **"Money does not tell me what to do. I tell money what to do."**

Now is your season to stop working for money, and make money work for you!

Have you ever gone to a restaurant and let money tell you what to do? You read the menu from right to left, checking the prices first.

But what if you made decisions based on what is truly important to you, your "why", instead of letting money dictate your choices? Shift your perspective and say, **"I'll create the money to make that happen."**

This is just a simple example, but for us, prosperity is not just about the number in your bank account. It's about blessing others, as we've said before. When we help others win, we win.

Wealth is not determined by the money in our bank account, but rather by the good intentions and deep desires in our hearts. That's why we're here, to amplify those desires and make a true impact on the world.

We want you to be as wealthy as possible because we know this is how we change the world. Say it with us, **"I will be wealthy for my why!"**

Let me, Chelsey, share a quick story with you about breaking the power of money over our lives and not letting it dictate how we spend it or how generous we can be.

Stephen and I have always had a huge desire to be generous from the very beginning, but during one of our slower seasons trading dollars for hours, we were feeling the weight of scarcity and letting the number in our bank account dictate how generous we could be. We knew we were onto something with Amazon, but we didn't want to be those people who said we'd be generous but didn't live it out. So, we decided to take out a scary amount of money from our bank account and give it away to friends and strangers. From that day forward, we made a rule in our house that it is always okay to be generous. We no longer ask money for permission to fulfill the calling in our lives, and we feel that one of our callings is to be radically generous.

We believe in the concept of "opposite greaters" where opposing forces are not equal, but one is greater than the other. For example, light is greater than darkness. **In a season where you're feeling stuck, sometimes investing in yourself or your business is an opposite greater act of breaking the power of scarcity over your life.** If you say you want financial freedom and time freedom, what are you doing about it? We believe what we do, not just what we say. We see people come to participate in these seven days and then quit, but we want you to be a doer who takes action and achieves their goals.

We're willing to invest in you and empower families with time and financial freedom, so much so that we've spent $241,000 in one of our recent challenges to get individuals just like you into the room to be able to hear this message.

We're playing the long game with you because when we help you win, you'll help us win.

Whether or not you decide to join our 12-month program, we want to say that **you are worth it**! We love you, and we care about you.

During a recent marketing meeting with someone outside our team, they asked us about the people we serve, and we got emotional talking about you and your breakthrough. We've been where you are, felt the same feelings, and we know what's possible. That's why we're convicted to share this message, because it's not just for us, it's for you.

All the stories you've heard this week, they're for you. We're willing to go down so you can go up because we believe in you!

THE "FAST PATH" TO WEALTH

Now, let's talk about the fast path to wealth. The first step is to **choose a vehicle to get you to your result**, and you've already found it - the Rainmaker Method.

Next, **follow one course until successful**. This is the biggest thing that holds people back from wealth – trying to do too many things. When you try to do too many things at once, it can be hard to make significant progress. There are many ways to make money, but you need to focus on one vehicle, and if you've chosen this one, follow one course until successful. Focus is key.

The third step is to **earn more than you spend, and then invest the difference**. It's a simple phrase, but it's a powerful concept. One of our wealth mentors taught us this, and we've found it to be true. And finally, remember that this is not just about you. Your breakthrough is for your kids, your grandkids, and beyond. It's about changing your family tree. That's powerful!

When you've made some money on Amazon, you honestly should reinvest some of it back into your Amazon business because you can get better returns on Amazon than with real estate, the stock market, or any other investment. But while I'm still reinvesting in Amazon, I'm also diversifying into other areas like real estate.

Don't fall for the myth that every millionaire has seven streams of income. In reality, most millionaires start with one source of income and then diversify once they've built it up. And for us, that one thing is Amazon. By focusing on the Rainmaker Method for a season, just one to two years, you can create generational wealth and achieve financial freedom.

Now, do you want to know the fastest path to wealth?

The answer is really simple – **get a mentor**. A mentor is someone who has paid the price so that you don't have to. They have gone through the challenges and can help guide you towards success.

There's a difference between a teacher and a mentor. A teacher can convey a topic well and help you understand it, but a mentor has real-life experience and can offer invaluable insights.

I, Stephen, remember walking to school in the snow with my friend Tyler and his older brother Ryan. He was bigger and made the steps in the snow, and all Tyler and I had to do was step in his footsteps. It made our journey to school a lot easier, and he knew the shortcuts that we didn't.

It's the same way with getting a mentor. You can go at it alone, but it's much easier to follow in the footsteps of someone who has already been there.

Yet, a good mentor isn't just someone who says, "Follow me." A good mentor is someone who says, "Why don't you go ahead now? You're ready to go ahead." A good mentor pushes you beyond your limits and helps you achieve even greater success than they have. That's what we strive for with our Rainmaker Program - not just to create results, but to send people off to succeed beyond even where we've been.

At Rainmakers, we believe in the power of mentoring. We have helped people achieve incredible success on Amazon, and we're honored to see them surpass our achievements. That's the kind of legacy we want to leave – empowering others to succeed and achieve more than we ever have.

Don't you want your kids to do more than you've ever done; succeed more than you ever have? That's our heart for Rainmakers, and that's the power of getting a mentor.

So if you're ready to achieve generational wealth, focus on Amazon and the Rainmaker Method for a short season of one to two years. Then, once you have grown your Amazon business, diversify your investments. But remember, you only need one thing to start: **a mentor**.

KEEPING YOUR EYE ON THE PRIZE

During our recent review of a video of our son Kai taking his first steps, it reminded me of the journey our Rainmakers, like you, are on. Just like Kai, you may be stepping into new territory!

There are three things I want to highlight from Kai's first steps that can apply to your journey as well:

First, **he kept his eye on the prize**. He was not looking left and right or down, but was focused on mommy and daddy and trying to wobble his way towards them. Similarly, it's important to keep your focus on your desired result and not get sidetracked.

Secondly, **when Kai fell down, he would pick himself up and keep going**. Many adults tend to quit after hitting one wall, but Kai enjoyed the process and kept trying. Don't give up after a setback, keep going and enjoy the journey.

Lastly, **Kai walked because he knew it was possible.** He had seen others walk and knew he could do it too. If you want to achieve success, it's important to surround yourself with people who have achieved it and see success as a normal thing. Surround yourself with a community of successful people who can show you what's possible.

To help you understand this journey better, let's use an analogy. Imagine you want to go from California to Hawaii:

- You could swim there, but it's dangerous and exhausting.

- You could try to do it on your own, but the journey would be rough. We've provided you with a boat to help you get there. It may still be challenging, but doable.

- You could take a plane, but it still involves going through security and checking your bags.

- Or, you could take a private jet, which is the easiest, fastest, and most enjoyable way to get there...

Which would you pick? Would you pick the private jet, above all the other options?

We have something for your Amazon business-building journey that's like a private jet, which can help you get to your desired result as fast as possible, and as easily as possible.

Would you like to find out more about this opportunity?

YOUR INVITATION: IT'S YOUR TIME!

Introducing our Rainmaker Mastermind - a coaching program that we've designed over the last 5 years to help you achieve your desired results.

What would it be like for you to have access to a hands-on approach to coaching, equipping you with the necessary training and supporting you every step of the way?

If you're currently still with us here on Day 5,
we invite you to join us for the rest of the journey at
www.rainmakerchallenges.com/apply

Complete your quick win for today by **inputting your name and email to unlock your Rainmaker application**.

Our program is designed for a select group of motivated Rainmakers who are committed to taking massive action and creating leverage in their lives. However, we have limited coaching capacity, so we do assess applications to ensure it's a good fit for both you and us. Coaching slots fill up fast, so apply as soon as possible.

When you join us, you'll gain access to a wealth of resources and support, including two months of our Product Research Accelerator Program with a Certified Rainmaker Coach who will be there to answer your questions. You'll also get a $10k payday guarantee, access to our community group for 12 months with daily coaching calls, and lifetime access to our fully unlocked app.

We're proud of what we've built in this mastermind, and we've encountered many obstacles along the way, equipping us with solutions for each one.

Our Rainmaker process will unlock who you become, which is a valuable skill set that will stay with you for a lifetime.

As you review our webpage, you'll see that we've included a seven-minute video that provides a quick overview of the program, as well as a detailed breakdown of the Rainmaker training portal. The portal is like an encyclopedia of everything you need to know to crush it on Amazon, and it's updated all the time!

One of the things that we're most proud of is our team. We hold team meetings every week with our core team, where we update the course content to better serve our students. We put our heads together to assess Amazon's changes and identify areas where our students need help, so we can create the content necessary to serve them at the highest level. When we asked you to dream with us, we wanted to know where you want to be financially a year from now. Every step of the way, we're thinking about how we can serve you better.

Amazon is changing constantly, but **instead of you spending time keeping up with it, our team takes care of that and updates the course material for you!**

But we don't stop there. Our program also includes real accountability. We don't just sell you a course and then leave you on your own. **Our coaches text you at least once a week to check in, see how you're doing, and hold you accountable to your goals.** This level of support makes all the difference. We had a student who fell off the map during COVID, but her coach reached out, turned things around, and helped her make $300,000 through her business.

This is why one of the most powerful features of our Rainmaker mastermind is **the full 2-month Product Research Accelerator**. You'll have access to an app on your phone or computer where you can send messages to a coach and an intimate cohort of Rainmakers in the same phase who will be there to support you. As mentioned previously, our coaches are experienced Amazon sellers who can help you navigate the product research phase quickly and avoid common pitfalls. They'll also hold you accountable by checking in with you at least once a week to ensure that you're taking steps toward your desired results.

In addition to the coaching, you'll also gain **access to our community group**, where you'll be surrounded by other amazing Rainmakers who are in the same process as you. This group is an awesome, positive environment where you can share wins, ask questions, and get support whenever you need it.

One of the most important additions to our program is **our daily coaching calls**, which we're incredibly proud of. From Monday to Friday, our Rainmakers have access to group coaching calls that they can join at any point during their journey. **Our coaching calls happen every day of the week, and they're all fully transcribed and searchable, which means that you can find what you need quickly and easily.**

Our team is deeply invested in your success and we believe that this level of accountability is essential for our students. Most coaching programs only offer one group call per week, but we wanted to make it even easier for our students to get help whenever they need it. We have separate calls for each phase of the process, and even allow you to submit questions in advance if you can't be there live. This level of coaching is usually only available at a much higher cost, but we wanted to make it accessible to all of our mastermind participants.

We understand that time is valuable, which is why we've included two powerful tools in our Rainmaker App. The first is **our Searchie integration**, which allows you to search through our entire archive of coaching calls. All of our coaching calls are transcribed and searchable, so you can find specific information quickly and easily. The second tool is **our Move the Needle Checklist**, which helps you visualize your progress through the course. You can move cards between columns to track your progress and even add your own checklist items.

We're always updating and improving these tools to make them more user-friendly and effective. Our ultimate goal is to equip you with the skills, knowledge, and tools you need to succeed on Amazon and beyond. With our Rainmaker Mastermind, you'll gain access to a wealth of resources and support that will help you achieve your desired result!

In addition to the coaching calls, you'll also receive **a fully unlocked Power Profit Tool** inside your app. This tool will help you with the promotion and advertising planning phases of your business, so you can stay on top of your numbers and ensure everything is checking out.

You'll also have access to our Product Qualifier Tool, which rates your product idea based on data and includes training videos to help you answer specific questions.

We'll also **provide you with pre-arranged sourcing and shipping partner connections**, as well as a ton of extra resources that are exclusively available to our mastermind members.

You'll even have **lifetime access to all future challenge replays**, so you can stay up to date with our latest content.

Lastly, you'll also have bonus access to **Stephen's Free Stuff Launch List, which has over 10,000 subscribers who love supporting business launches on Amazon**. You can send an email to our list when you launch a product and do a promotion or discount to drive attention to it. We'll give your product attention on Facebook and help get it to the front page of Amazon.

We want you to be 100% successful, so our team will write your first product listing entirely for you. We'll also provide calls devoted to product research and help you identify the best keywords to use on Amazon.

We offer other free bonuses when you join, such as **an onboarding mini-course, daily coaching, a 60-minute business consultation, and a complimentary done-for-you LLC consultation.**

To recap, our program is comprehensive, and we're committed to helping you succeed. Our team is dedicated to updating the course content to better serve you, and we offer coaching, accountability, and a supportive community.

Go to **www.rainmakerchallenges.com/apply** to continue journeying with us into the creation of your successful and profitable business. With our program, you'll have everything you need to succeed on Amazon!

What's Included When You Join The
Rainmaker Mastermind

✓ **Lifetime Access to Rainmaker Method Training Portal**

 Daily Group Coaching Calls So You Never Get Stuck

 12mo Community Access

 Access to Rainmaker Milestone Awards

 Move The Needle Tool To Stay In Momentum Daily

 Complimentary LLC Consultation & Discounted LLC Entity Creation

 2 Months Personalized Coaching Accelerator Group

 "Done FOR You" Product Listing Search Engine Optimizing (Listing SEO)

 Access to The 11-Point Product Qualifier Tool For Instant Product Feedback

 Pre-Arranged Sourcing Agent & Shipping Partner Connections

 Unlimited Access To StephensFreeStuff Launch Service

 Rainmaker App Future Upgrades & Features & Tools

 24/7 AI Coach "Raina" Access

 How To Raise $50k Without Asking Anyone For Money

 $10k Pay Day Guarantee - Take Action & Make $10k Or We Pay You $10k

 Fully Unlocked Power Profit Tool V3

 Surprise Guest Expert Trainers & Mentors in Mastermind Group

And More....

Total Value: **$74,850+**

Think about it - what would it be worth to you to have a recurring, reliable, recession-proof income stream for your family within just one year of signing up? What if you could create generational wealth within two to three years? We know of no other vehicle that can do that, based on our experience.

Here's a recap of what's included in our Rainmaker mastermind program:

- Seven weekly Coaching Clinics that cover different phases of the business

- Product Research Accelerator Group Coaching for the first two months

- Weekly Accountability Check-ins, Onboarding Team and 24/7 email support

- Guest trainers

- Access to all Rainmaker Tools and Members-only Resources

- Listing writing service and SEO optimization

- Access to launch service and Container Concierge service

- Rainmaker warehouse access

- 24/7 AI Coach "Raina" Access

- Product Qualifier Tool with training videos

- Lifetime access to all future challenge replays

- Free bonuses such as an onboarding mini-course and LLC consultation

The total value of these services is $74,000 USD, but the best part is...

You don't have to pay $74,000 to join our Rainmaker Mastermind!

It's an investment that is a fraction of what people pay for franchises or higher education. And yet, the secrets to building wealth and financial freedom are within your grasp.

Don't fall into the trap of believing in limited resources. The cost of not taking action now is much greater than the investment you'll make in the Rainmaker mastermind. If you're serious about achieving financial freedom, then you need to take this opportunity to work with us.

Joining the Rainmaker Mastermind means access to seven coaching clinics each week, the Product Research Accelerator with a Rainmaker coach for the initial two months, weekly accountability, complimentary LLC consultation, and so much more. You'll also receive all our powerful tools, members-only resources, and lifetime access to future challenge replays.

Yet again, it's not just about the tools and resources - it's also about the community. You'll have access to six- and seven-figure sellers who can hold you accountable, guest trainers and teachers who will share their top techniques for selling better than 90% of all Amazon sellers, and daily coaching clinics to support you throughout your journey.

So what are you waiting for? **Join our Rainmaker mastermind today and start building your passive income business!** You'll be amazed at the results you can achieve in just a few short months. Let us help you unlock the secrets of building wealth and financial freedom – put in your application now at **www.rainmakerchallenges.com/apply**.

OUR CRAZY AMAZING $10K GUARANTEE

At Rainmakers, we believe in generosity and unpredictable surprises. We have a crazy idea for those who are action-takers, and we want to share it with you. We know you've heard of the 30-day money-back guarantee before, but we think it rewards inaction. In the Western world, we tend to believe that buying something means we've achieved it, but in the Eastern world, they know that the real achievement comes from actually doing it.

We don't want you to invest in Rainmakers without a Western mindset, only to be unwilling to take action and change your life forever. If that sounds like you, then please do not apply. We care about the success of our students, and we believe that if you have success, we have success too. That's why when we invest in you, we want you to be all-in to reach the Benjamin Club, which means earning $100 a day and beyond.

Working with us for 30 days, only to have you change your mind costs a lot of our time, money, and resources.

If you've made it this far, you're committed to this process. You have the time for this business. You know your why, and you're already determined. Maybe you've even invested in software tools like Helium 10, or you're already doing this thing, and you've seen how we over-deliver on promises. We love to solve problems in our community, and we, as Rainmakers, create solutions for any problem that comes up!

Let's say you take the Rainmaker Personal Responsibility Challenge and complete it. You can join this full experience for a fraction of the price. This offer is all-in, which means you're personally responsible for taking action. This can be scary, but we believe in you, and we're here to support you.

Instead of a 30-day money-back guarantee that rewards indecisiveness, we're offering the $10k Payday Guarantee. If you don't make $10k at minimum, we'll pay you $10k. Since we launched this guarantee, so many Rainmakers have thrived. It's a scary guarantee for us to launch, but we're truthful and honest about our processes, and we have checkpoints for our Rainmakers.

If you follow those checkpoints outlined in the Rainmaker Method and launch a product within the first six months, we guarantee you'll make $10k in revenue within your first year or we'll reimburse you up to $5k of your Rainmaker investment and purchase back from you any unsold inventory up to $5k. We built in these safeguards to catch you and put you back up on the edge of the plane you're building.

In essence, there's literally no risk in this business, and our goal is to reduce risk in every phase of it. This is the ultimate, no-risk guarantee - our $10k Payday Guarantee. We believe in the Rainmaker Method, and we believe in you. If you have gotten this far in this 7-day process, we're willing to take that risk completely on our shoulders because we believe you're good soil.

This is the right plant, right place moment – let's grow something beautiful for your family.

YOUR RAINMAKERS
APPLICATION WALKTHROUGH

Are you ready to embark on an incredible journey towards becoming a Rainmaker and achieving a lifestyle of time freedom and financial overflow for your family?

If so, welcome to our Rainmakers Application Process, where we'll walk you step by step through the simple process towards joining our incredible community.

To begin, you'll start on our case study opt-in page here at
www.rainmakerchallenges.com/apply

Here, you'll have the opportunity to access a valuable short case study that showcases the power of our Rainmaker program. **Simply click on the "Get Your Case Study" button** and enter your name, email, and phone number.

Once you've gotten to the next page, **click "View Case Study" to watch the impactful video**. This case study is designed to help you gain a deeper understanding of what awaits you, so we highly recommend you watch it!

After watching the case study, it's time to take your next step and **click on the "Apply" button**. This will lead you to the application form where you'll answer a series of questions. Take your time to provide thoughtful and accurate responses, as this information will help us better understand your goals and aspirations. Once you've completed the application, you'll arrive at a page congratulating you on qualifying for a complimentary one-on-one strategy session.

Now, it's time to **book your strategy session**. Choose a time that works best for you from the available options. Don't forget to click "Done" at the bottom of the page to finalize your booking!

On this page, you'll also find two important videos. The first is a thank you video that provides valuable insights on how to make the most out of your upcoming call. The second video is a bonus training that offers a comprehensive overview of our program, answering any lingering questions you may have and ensuring you're fully prepared for your strategy session.

With all the necessary preparations complete, all that's left is for you to **show up ready for a breakthrough during your strategy session**!

Our team of experienced strategists are excited to connect with you, understand your unique situation, and provide tailored guidance to set you on the path to success.

We're thrilled to have you take this journey with us. Our Rainmaker family is ready to support you every step of the way. Get ready to unlock your potential and create the life of your dreams through your Amazon business!

CONGRATULATIONS!
YOU'VE MADE IT THIS FAR...

Congratulations on making it through your first 5 days in the Family Freedom Challenge! To celebrate your progress, you'll receive a badge on the Thank You Page once you complete your application. We encourage you to post it in the Facebook group so that we can all celebrate with you!

This challenge has given you a taste of what it's like to work with us, and if you feel that this is a good fit for you, we invite you to work with us for the long term. Let's take action, hold each other's hands, and be people who do what we say we believe in. Let's stretch ourselves and think differently, even when it's scary.

We understand that investing in yourself can be daunting, but it's okay to feel those emotions. We understand how it feels, and we've been there ourselves. We invest heavily in ourselves, and it has paid off with returns far beyond our initial investments.

Last year, Chelsey and I invested $125,000 in personal training, education, and mentorship. We didn't start there, but rather worked our way up. And now, the knowledge and skills we acquired have trickled down to you through our podcast and other resources. We had to push past our fears and say yes to the opportunities that presented themselves to us.

For example, when we first said yes to joining a $50,000 mastermind, there were tears and emotions, and we almost let fear get in the way. But this mastermind changed our lives and opened up new opportunities for us.

You might be feeling nervous or scared, but those are just emotions. We've learned to reframe those feelings as excitement for the possibilities ahead.

We promise to have your back, and our $10k Payday Guarantee takes away all the risk.... but ultimately, you will still need to take action and run this race.

And as you take action, we will cheer you on, give you feedback, hold you accountable, and be with you every step of the way, helping you take one step at a time towards your goals.

Congratulations again on completing the first week of this challenge!

Tomorrow's chapter will be a "Funding Clinic" where you'll learn how to gain the funding you may need to start your Amazon business.

THE
Rainmaker
MANIFESTO

I am a RAINMAKER.
Part of the innovative few who are creating systems
to **buy back our time**.
I step into an abundance that empowers
and enables me to **pour more into my WHY**.
I don't work for money, I make my money work for me.
I take immediate action on any opportunity
to make it rain for my family, for my children, **for my legacy.**
I am decisive & committed,
outsourcing my weaknesses and focusing on my strengths.
I take calculated risks, taking steps that stretch myself **daily**.
In a world run by fear, I overcome and feel alive.
Like a diamond, **pressure is my unfair advantage**
to produce something valuable.
As Rainmakers, we support one another.
We believe in **community over competition** and share what we learn.
I have power and authority over my finances
and will **change lives through my generosity**.
Above all, I remain true to my WHY.
Success is not luck, **success is a choice**.
Yesterday, today and tomorrow, I've made my choice.
I am a Rainmaker.

THE
Rainmaker
FAMILY

DAY 5's
QUICK WIN:

UNLOCK YOUR RAINMAKERS APPLICATION

Are you tired of feeling stuck in your current financial situation? Do you dream of creating a successful business that provides financial freedom for you and your family?

Today's Quick Win is to go now to
www.rainmakerchallenges.com/apply
to unlock your Rainmaker's application and take the first step towards becoming a part of our exclusive Rainmaker Mastermind.

Our expert coaches and community are here to provide you with the tools and support you need to turn your dreams into a reality.

Don't let fear hold you back any longer. Join us today and let's work together to make your Amazon business goals a reality!

Rainmaker Family Challenge!

Six Figure Roadmap

Today Stephen & Chelsey will be breaking down the step by step process to the **#1 secret** to success when it comes to your Rainmaker Business Imagine making anywhere from $100-1000/day.

Today's Action Steps:

☐ Step One	☐ Step Two
Read **Day Five's** training	Apply to the **Rainmaker Mastermind**

Are you ready? Let's get started!

Rainmaker

#CELEBRATIONS

Rainmaker Melissa:

"As a busy mother of seven with other businesses and mission work in Central America, I never thought I'd have the time or resources to pursue yet another venture.

Yet, the need for more monthly income was pressing. So when the opportunity to join Rainmakers presented itself, I decided to give it a shot, despite having zero knowledge of Amazon FBA.

I was overwhelmed at first and struggled to grasp the concepts, but I kept at it, and eventually things started to click. I did product research for one or two hours each night after the kids were asleep, and *eventually launched a product that quickly sold out and made it into the Benjamin Club, bringing in $100 a day within the first month.*

From there, we launched two more products and have two more on the way, with sales rapidly approaching $100,000 within one year of starting our Amazon business. It's been a journey of ups and downs, and we even sold a car to invest in the business at one point, but the results have been worth it!

So if you're feeling overwhelmed and uncertain, just remember that it's possible to succeed in this business with persistence and determination. Don't give up, and keep pushing through!"

10

DAY SIX: FUNDING YOUR FUTURE

What would it be like for you if you were part of a community where success is normalized and financial freedom is achievable?

At Rainmakers, we believe in equipping our members with the resources they need to turn their big dreams into reality.

That's why on Day 6, we want to focus on funding and specifically, how to overcome any financial barriers holding you back from joining our program. We understand that money can be a big obstacle for some, but we don't want it to be the wall that prevents you from working with us.

We know that sometimes it takes a shift in thinking to achieve success, especially when it comes to finances. If you don't want to be average or normal, you can't just take mainstream advice when it comes to finances because you don't desire to live an average life. This is what will create a bank account for you that isn't average in the days ahead either!

When you've taken steps of faith to choose to be an entrepreneur, sometimes you have to do things differently.

This is why we want to work with you further and invite you to join our mastermind community. We're proud of the success stories and transformed lives that have come out of our program, and we believe it can do the same for you.

We understand that we're working hard to get you into our program, but it's because we believe it's the best path to financial freedom. Think of it as taking a private jet to your dream destination rather than taking a swim or boat. We want fthe best for you, and we're committed to empowering you with the resources you need to make it happen.

Today, we want to share a resource with you that has helped many Rainmakers in our community start their businesses and raise over $5 million collectively. The truth is, traditional banks and financial institutions often don't understand the unique challenges that entrepreneurs face, especially moms who are starting their own businesses on platforms like Amazon. We understand these challenges, and that's why we're here to share this resource with you.

We believe in transparency and sharing our setbacks as well as our successes. This is because we've been in your shoes before, and we know what it's like to have the wrong mindset about funding and money.

In fact, we made some mistakes early on in our Amazon business journey when we were also going through Dave Ramsey's Financial Peace University Program.

While Dave Ramsey has great advice for the average person who has a 9 to 5 job, his teachings don't always apply to entrepreneurs who need to think differently about money and business opportunities. We learned this lesson the hard way when we put all our family's cash flow into paying off our house instead of investing in our Amazon business. This decision caused our Amazon business to stall, and we couldn't continue to grow our business due to a lack of capital.

If we had the knowledge and tools that we're sharing with you today, our

Amazon business would have continued to grow and flourish. That's why we're excited to share with you the secret of leveraging OPM - Other People's Money! We understand that money and funding can be intimidating, but with the right knowledge and mindset shift, you can overcome these obstacles and make your business dreams a reality!

Many people come into our community with old mindsets about money and funding, influenced by lies they have been told. However, our Rainmaker funding options have helped many Rainmakers have personal experiences with funding in a positive manner that protects their family's cash flow. We will be sharing expertise and insights to help you shift your mindset about funding and understand how it can be a valuable tool for your business.

We want you to be open to this powerful resource because we know how it feels to be stuck with a business idea due to lack of funding. With our expertise and support, you can be empowered to start on your journey towards succeeding as an entrepreneur.

"Money is a terrible master, but an excellent servant."

As entrepreneurs, we need to shift our mindset and understand that money is a tool. The truth is that you don't need to fear money or debt, but you do need to **learn how to leverage and use debt** *so that* money serves you, and you can serve others.

Now, let me ask you this question... Is debt always bad?

We want to be sensitive to this question because we understand that you may have been raised with a conservative mindset around money, just like we were.

As an entrepreneur, it is essential to differentiate between personal and business finances, and while Dave Ramsey's approach can be fantastic for personal finances (keyword being "personal"), we need to think like business owners when it comes to starting and growing a business.

Personal debt is taking on debt with no expectation of a greater return, like purchasing a TV, whereas **business debt** is taking on debt with an educated expectation of a greater return.

It's crucial to understand the difference and make informed decisions.

Good debt means taking on debt with an educated expectation of a greater return, just like companies such as Amazon, Under Armour, and Google have done. These companies leveraged debt at an early stage of their business, and their success speaks for itself.

Now, we know that most of us here are trying to change our lives and provide for our families, and for that, we need to figure out a way to maximize our returns.

For instance, let's take two clients - Client A and Client B. Client A invested $2,000 in inventory in January and reinvested their 15% profit every month resulting in a return of $8700 in a year. While that may seem like a great return, for most of us, it's not enough to make a significant impact.

On the other hand, client B invested $15,000 using the same model, and their return is now worth $65,254. This is still not a crazy amount of money, but it can allow you to spend more time with your family and focus on growing your business.

So, even a small investment and a modest profit margin of 15% can make a difference in growing your business and achieving your goals.

As an entrepreneur, you need to think about how you can **leverage other people's money to take your business to the next level**.

This includes using 0% interest loans to purchase inventory, investing in coaching and mentorship, paying for marketing and software, attending events and trainings, and even consolidating high-interest credit card debt.

THE FINANCIAL CAPITAL LADDER

To help you better understand your funding options, it's important to familiarize yourself with the Financial Capital Ladder.

This ladder includes various funding solutions available to businesses, and entrepreneurs must know where they stand and what funding opportunities they can pursue in the future.

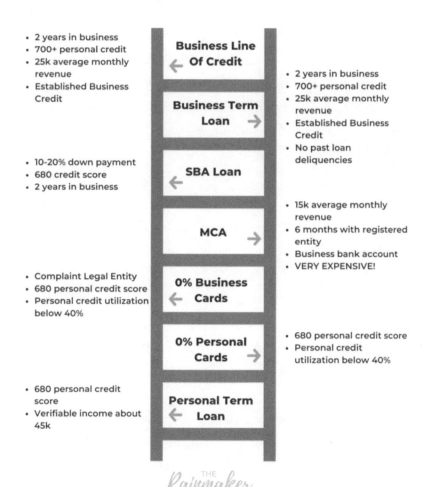

Just to note, we generally advise against merchant cash advances (MCA) unless it's the only option to stay in business because they can be very expensive.

It's important to keep these requirements in mind, so you don't waste time pursuing funding options that aren't a good fit for your business's current stage.

OUR RECOMMENDATION FOR AMAZON BUSINESS OWNERS

A question that we always get from Amazon business owners is, "What funding is right for me?" And as someone who comes from an Amazon business background, I can confidently say that **revolving credit** is a number #1 key.

The first reason for this is credit-based approvals. As entrepreneurs and 1099 contractors, it can be difficult to show our income or provide collateral, but with revolving credit like a 0% interest business card, you don't have to worry about that.

The second reason is that it's an inventory-driven business. With revolving credit, you can do your research, determine what products will sell, and then make buying decisions accordingly. You only make payments when you use the money, whereas, with a loan, you'll have to make payments even if you don't use the funds.

The third reason is that it's open-ended. As you pay down your revolving line of credit, you can spend and pay it down again repeatedly. This is great for an inventory-driven business where you'll be buying inventory over and over again.

Fourth, you'll get 0% interest for 12 to 18 months with every funding product on the revolving side. I have yet to find a 0% interest loan, even something like a home equity line is still at least 6%.

Last but not least, our favorite reason is the cashback, bonuses, and points that you can earn. For Amazon businesses, this is free inventory. You can use these cards for all your business spending, marketing, travel, and everything in between.

So for those of you who are really serious about growing your business, and want to see what type of funding you qualify for, simply go to our website at **www.rainmakerchallenges.com/apply**.

If you KNOW this is what you want to do, and you just need to figure out the HOW...

Our team is amazing at doing this, helping you see what would work for you, and coming up with creative ways to fund you fast!

OUR RAINMAKER CASE STUDIES

What would it be like for you if you were able to overcome the common roadblock of limited resources and tap into a whole world of funding opportunities?

Imagine being able to access funding without ever having to ask anyone for money, and having the skills and knowledge to make money quickly and easily through various channels. How would that change your business and your life?

It's time to break free from the illusion of limited resources and start leveraging the abundance of resources available to you, as you've just discovered.

For the rest of this chapter, we want to remind you of the opportunities that await when you choose to continue this journey with us inside of our Rainmaker mastermind. Here are a handful of Rainmaker case studies to inspire and encourage you to keep taking action towards what's possible.

When you join our 12-month program through
www.rainmakerchallenges.com/apply
you gain access to everything we've shared yesterday and extra bonuses like:

- How to raise $50,000 without ever asking anyone for money

- How to make $200 to $1,000 with just your cell phone camera

- How to earn referral bonuses of up to $833 just by sharing your Rainmaker journey

- And more.

We even have a section of the course dedicated to "make money now" ideas to help you overcome any limiting beliefs about resources.

When you join our Rainmaker mastermind, you're joining a community of like-minded individuals who are dedicated to helping each other succeed. Our ongoing support and guidance will ensure you keep the momentum going beyond the sprint of this challenge!

1. Rainmaker Scarleth:

"Hey! I'm Scarleth, and I am a proud Rainmaker! Two years ago, I started the challenge with no hope of joining Rainmakers. But one Saturday, 7-Figure Funding gave us an opportunity, and my life changed forever.

My husband and I are missionaries in Honduras, and we had lost a lot of businesses due to the pandemic. We were hopeless and thought that we could never start a new business again. But my coach invited me to the challenge, and even though I didn't speak English, she encouraged me to take the leap. I was scared, and I didn't think I could do it, but my coach and my husband believed in me. So, we jumped in, and we were approved to join the Rainmaker Mastermind.

I can't believe how much my life has changed since becoming a Rainmaker. We launched our first product with the help of 7-Figure Funding, and everything went well. The Rainmaker Family also taught us how to make money in other ways, and six months after joining, I made a profit of $100,000. Now, I only need one to two hours a day to check my business, and I even took another job just because I wanted to. The Rainmaker community changed my mindset, and I am no longer negative or have a poverty mindset. Now, I can travel and enjoy my time with my family because I have credit and points to use. I am free, and I can spend my time doing what I love.

If you are hesitant about joining Rainmakers, I understand. I was there too, but the Rainmaker Mastermind taught me everything I needed to know. It will change your life, and I can guarantee that you will never be the same person again. Just remember your why and put in the effort, and everything will work out."

2. Rainmaker Sharon:

"Hey guys, Rainmaker Sharon here. Let me tell you a little story about my journey. When my daughter was just four weeks old, she wouldn't breastfeed, so I was exclusively pumping. My husband was a videographer, and Stephen was a wedding videographer too, thank God. One day, Stephen made a post, I commented on it, and that's how it all started.

From that point on in 2017, I just kept pushing. I chose to quit my job as a nurse, which was hard because I really loved it. But now, I get to work on my own time and do my own thing!

When I started my business, I barely had any money to start. There was no funding, all I had was a pen and paper, and I had to stand on the street and beg for money to start this thing. But I didn't let that stop me.

Now, I've sold 78 units of my product today. And if we look at the past year, I've done $1.3 million. This year alone, I've earned $845,000 in the US, $43,000 in Canada, and £27,000 in the UK. I've never even been to Canada or the UK!

But my journey wasn't easy. I've had 17 pregnancies, and I kept having miscarriages, which landed me in the hospital. So every year, I only got to work for about eight months, and the other four months, I *was in the hospital. It's been a revolving cycle, but in 2017, when I finally had my first daughter after six miscarriages, I knew I had to take a risk and put my heart into it. I ordered my second product for $3,600, and when it got here, I couldn't sell it because I didn't have a special permit. But I didn't let that stop me. I kept pushing and looking for my third product.*

And the reason why I love doing this challenge is that you get bombarded with a lot of ads. Most of them are doctored, and people doctor their stuff. But here, you can see that it's real. It's not plug and play, but if you have a coach and a community, it makes things a lot easier. We're all approachable, and there's always someone who has been there before you and can help you fix your mistakes."

So to answer the question of whether you should do it or not, my answer is, "Why not?"

Don't let the fear of failure stop you from taking a risk and chasing your dreams. You never know where it might lead you.

PREPARING FOR TOMORROW

At this point in this book, we've discussed what you want: time freedom, financial freedom, and why you want it. We've delved deep into your motivation and the importance of understanding who you need to become in order to achieve your goals.

Entrepreneurship and becoming a Rainmaker require an identity shift and building something that lasts. While the financial results and time freedom are amazing, the process of becoming a Rainmaker is equally powerful, and we need to celebrate it every step of the way. That's why we celebrate you and have awards in our Mastermind to acknowledge your progress.

Don't fall into the trap of thinking that happiness and satisfaction only come when you reach a specific financial goal. Enjoy the process, and measure yourself backward and forward to see how far you've come.

Look how far you've come in this challenge. You've come so far, and who you've become even this week is so powerful. Let's continue that momentum. Imagine where you'll be in a year, five years, or ten years from now, if you keep pushing forward and keep stepping into your potential. The possibilities are endless!

YOUR DAY 6
QUICK WIN:

HAVE YOU SUBMITTED YOUR RAINMAKERS APPLICATION?

Imagine a life where financial freedom is no longer a dream, but a reality... If you're feeling stuck in your current situation and envision creating a successful business, then it's time to take action.

Start by submitting your Rainmaker's application at **www.rainmakerchallenges.com/apply** and take the first step towards becoming a part of our exclusive Rainmaker Mastermind!

With our expert coaches and community, you'll have access to the tools and support needed to make your dreams a reality.

If you KNOW this is what you want to do, and you just need to figure out the HOW, our team can help you find creative ways that do just that.

Don't let fear hold you back any longer.

Join us today and then go to our Rainmakers FB Group to let us know with #familyfreedombook so we can all celebrate with you.

Let's work together to make your Amazon business goals a reality!

Rainmaker Family Challenge!

DAY SIX
Funding Your Future

Today's Training is all about stepping into the **How Can I**, mindset and getting resourceful to Fund Your Rainmaker Future.

Today's Action
Steps:

☐ Step One	☐ Step Two	☐ Step Three
Read **Day Six's** training	Review Your **#FBAFund** Tracker, and share your updated tracker in the FB Group	Apply to the **Rainmaker Mastermind**

Are you ready? Let's get started!

Rainmaker
#CELEBRATIONS

Rainmaker Aubrey May:

"My whole life I wanted to be a teacher and after being one and having kids, I realized I couldn't let go of my babies! So we decided for me to quit my job and become a one income family. But I also found at the same time that I'm a really passionate person and I love having my own creative outlet.

So I tried a little bit of everything. I dabbled in photography, but my daughter wouldn't take a bottle so I couldn't really leave her to do photo sessions. I tried MLMs, but it's very much trading dollars for hours. We've tried lots of real estate things. Ultimately we just really wanted to dive into that passive income thing.

As soon as I found Rainmakers I knew this was the next thing for our family and I went straight for the Mastermind. I found my first two products in the spring and they consistently made $10,000 a month.

One day I was on Instagram clicking through and this influencer mentioned that there's this hole in the market. So I messaged her and I said, 'Hey, what if I could bring this to market and make it accessible to all these mamas? Would you like to collaborate with me?' She agreed and we dove in deep. The really cool thing is that not only was this next step going to transform my life, but it was about to change my sister's life as well.

We had a choice that we had to make. Would we do this on our own or invite my sister into this opportunity? We decided to go in together with her and we launched an incredible brand whose products sold out in a few short hours. We sold $40,000 on our first day! The day we restocked we did another $43,000 in sales and sold out again! I didn't hold anything back, but decided to take that leap and go all in. Because I said yes to this opportunity I not only am changing my family's financial future, but my sister's as well!"

11

DAY SEVEN: SETTING UP YOUR AMAZON SELLER ACCOUNT

Today, we're going to dive into setting up your Amazon Seller account.

Now, we want to start by giving you a bit of a backstory to understand why it's a little bit tricky. Amazon is a massive opportunity, and where there's a lot of money to be made, there's also a lot of attention: good and bad. Just like pirates during the height of ocean trade, there are also scammers, hijackers, and fake accounts on Amazon.

That's why Amazon has made this process a little bit challenging for anyone to get started. But, fear not, we're here to guide you through it all so this becomes a breeze for you.

GETTING THROUGH THE DOCUMENTATION HURDLE WITH EASE

Now, Amazon might ask for documentation to verify that you're a real human being living in the country you're trying to sell in. Typically, they'll ask for personal identification, like a driver's license or passport, and one other form of identification, like a bank statement or utility bill to prove you have access to addresses in the United States.

Amazon has three methods of verification:

- Method 1 is the most common, where they'll ask you to **upload those two documents**. I'll share some tips on how to do this effectively.

- Method 2 is **a postcard in the mail** with a code that you'll enter on the site. It's huge, and it's easy to get approved if you receive this method.

- Method 3 is **a video call interview** where they'll make sure you're human and ask to see your documents. This method is experimental, but some Rainmakers have been successful with it.

About 75% of people can sign up for an Amazon seller account and get in right away without being asked for verification documents. The other 25% will be asked to upload documentation. If you're an international Rainmaker wanting to sell in the USA, there are a few extra steps you have to take. If you join our Mastermind program there is a comprehensive guide that will aid you through that whole process.

Amazon's verification process may seem daunting, but it's in place to protect their customers. Unfortunately, there are people out there who create fake accounts and sell fake products to make a quick buck, compromising the integrity of the platform. By verifying the identity of sellers, Amazon ensures that only legitimate businesses are allowed to sell on their platform, giving customers peace of mind and protecting their trust in the brand. So, while the process may seem tedious, it's ultimately for the benefit of everyone involved, and a necessary step towards becoming a successful seller on Amazon.

TIPS TO EXPERIENCE A SMOOTH VERIFICATION PROCESS

Tip 1: Serve *with* Amazon!

Whenever any issue arises, frame it in a way that shows you're on their team to serve their customers. This goes a long way in your communication with Amazon.

Tip 2: Have high-quality scanned documents.

Amazon is looking out for potential scammers and fake accounts, so make sure your documents look genuine. One way to do this is to print out your bank statement and then fold it in thirds before scanning it back into your computer. This makes it look like an authentic document that hasn't been manipulated. You can block off any sensitive information on the statement with a sharpie.

To submit a full-page scan of your driver's license or passport, place the document in the corner of a piece of paper and scan the whole page, making sure to submit both sides of your driver's license. And don't forget to double-check the requirements for uploading documents before submitting. The requirements for uploading documents include submitting a JPEG file that is under 10 MB.

When scanning, make sure to use a good, quality scanner or camera with good lighting, preferably near a window. If your document is of poor quality or low light, Amazon may deny your application, but don't worry as you can always appeal the denial and fix the issue.

Tip 3: Avoid having multiple Amazon seller accounts, especially under the same roof.

Amazon is strict when it comes to multiple accounts as it may give the impression that the seller is attempting to manipulate the system by giving themselves reviews. Amazon tracks the IP address of the accounts and is always on the lookout for suspicious activities. Hence, it's essential to check with others living in the same household and avoid logging in to Amazon seller accounts from the same IP address.

In case you already have an Amazon seller account, it's best to start with that one instead of creating a new account. However, if Amazon informs you that your account has expired and to set up a new account, you should take a screenshot of the message and use it as proof if you encounter any issues later.

However, if you've been approved by Amazon to set up a second account, such as for a separate brand, it's possible to do so with Amazon's permission. Some Rainmakers do this after launching one brand to keep another brand completely separate. If you receive approval for a second account, make sure to keep the approval in writing from Amazon.

Tip 4: Make sure everything matches.

When it comes to uploading documents for your Amazon seller account, it's important to make sure that everything matches. This is the number one thing that the team responsible for approving accounts checks for, and they only have a few seconds to make a decision.

You can imagine them sitting at their desks, with a giant "no" button and a tiny "yes" button, and only a few seconds to make their decision! That's why everything needs to match perfectly. Amazon does everything on timers, and saving even a few seconds can mean millions of dollars for a company of this size.

So, to make it easy for the Amazon team to say "yes" to your account, the easiest ones to match are **a passport or driver's license as an identity document, and a bank statement or utility bill as proof of address**. Remember to make sure everything matches, including your name, address, and any other relevant details. If you've just moved or changed your name, update your documents before setting up your Amazon account.

Tip 5: Get through the gate *first*, and then make changes later!

It's important to remember that all of this information can be changed later. You can change your business name, email, and even transfer ownership to a different person or entity.

So if you already have an LLC, you'll be using your EIN Number. But if you're just starting out as a sole proprietor, then you'll want to set it up using your social security number. I'd recommend starting with your social security number first and transitioning to an LLC later if you're bootstrapping this. However, if you're in our mastermind, we have a program that will help you set up an LLC and obtain an EIN Number.

The key is to get approved and then make any necessary changes after the fact.

Whenever you make changes, it's a good idea to document everything and communicate with the Seller Central Team. This will help prevent any potential glitches or issues down the road. So if there are any denials or questions, you can provide proof of your communication and have a record of your previous interactions.

BONUS TOOL TUTORIAL:
THE JOTNOT SCANNING APP

Let's talk about how to use the JotNot App to scan your documents!

First, hit the "Scan" button at the bottom of the screen, and your camera will pop up. Make sure you're in good lighting and hover over the document you want to scan until the app creates a box around it.

Then take the photo, and if the corners aren't perfect, hit back to edit them until they're aligned.

Next, hit "process" in the upper right-hand corner, and change the black and white filter to color or photo, depending on your preference. Lastly, hit "save" and name your document something simple without spaces, like your driver's license number.

For your bank statement, print it out and fold it in thirds, then scan it back in using the same process. This will make it look like it came in the mail and more legitimate. Once you've scanned all of your documents, double-check everything and hit cancel for now. You'll do the front and back of your driver's license and select "document down below" to choose whether to upload a bank statement or credit card statement.

After you've submitted your documents, Amazon will review your account, which can take anywhere from a few hours to a couple of weeks.

Don't worry if you don't hear back right away. If your account is not approved, don't give up. Respond back and double-check your documents. Amazon may make mistakes, so don't be afraid to fight it. Just keep uploading documents and providing more information until you get approved!

CHOOSING YOUR BUSINESS'S NAME

Let's discuss your business name. Have you come up with a business name for your company after going through our book's challenge this week?

As we mentioned, on Amazon, you have a storefront name, which is the name you see at the top of the page when you walk into a physical store. However, within the store, there are multiple brands, and Amazon allows you to have multiple brands within your storefront.

So don't worry about creating specific brand names just yet. You can do that later when you know what products you'll be selling.

For now, when it comes to your business name, I recommend making it more broad and expandable. Choose a storefront name that can be applicable to a range of products, rather than something too niche or specific, unless that's what you're going for.

To come up with your business name, you might want to do a quick search on Amazon to see if anyone is already using that name. You can do this by typing in the name and checking if any results pop up. If there are no results, that's a good sign, but it's not enough to ensure that the name is unique.

Next, you can do a Google search for the name in parentheses to see if any brand names come up. Again, if you don't see any brand names, that's great, but it's still not a guarantee that the name is unique.

The last step is to do a trademark search. You can do this by visiting the U.S. Patent and Trademark Office (USPTO) website and clicking on "Search our trademark database." From there, you can do a basic word search and see if any trademarks with the name you've chosen come up. If there are no records found, then you're good to go!

However, if you do find existing trademarks with the same name, don't panic. Trademarks only apply to specific industries, so as long as you're not selling something similar to what the existing trademarks cover, you should be fine. But if you're unsure, it's always best to consult with a trademark lawyer or specialist.

In any case, if you're worried about potential conflicts, you can always make your name more unique. Maybe you can add a prefix or suffix to it or remove some letters to make it stand out. Just make sure it's still easy to pronounce and remember.

Keep in mind that the most important thing is to get your business up and running, so don't let choosing a name hold you back. Choose a name that fits your brand and vision, and let's get started!

NOW FOR YOUR FINAL STEPS

To set up your Amazon Seller account, let us share with you some tricks that will make the process easier. First, go to amazon.com and scroll down to the bottom until you see the "Make Money with Us" section. Click on the "Sell Products On Amazon" option.

Back to top

Make Money with Us

Sell products on Amazon

Sell apps on Amazon

Supply to Amazon

Protect & Build Your Brand

Become an Affiliate

Become a Delivery Driver

Amazon Payment Products

Amazon Visa

Amazon Store Card

Amazon Secured Card

Amazon Business Card

Shop with Points

Credit Card Marketplace

Reload Your Balance

Once you are navigated to the next page, don't click on the sign-up button just yet.

Amazon offers two types of accounts: the individual seller account and the professional account. While the latter offers more support and unlimited selling, it comes with a monthly fee of $39.99 (at the time of this writing).

When you get to this page, scroll all the way down to the bottom and click on "Just have a few items to sell? Sign up to become an individual seller."

For those of you who are still in the product research phase, we recommend signing up for the individual seller account. It's a free account, but you will be charged $1 per item sold. It's an excellent option to test the waters and start selling a few items. But once you plan to sell more than 40 units per month, it's best to upgrade to the professional account to avoid paying additional fees.

It's important to know the tips we're about to share, so you can avoid getting your account denied and save yourself some trouble!

The second step is to create an Amazon Seller account. There are two different options to sign up for the Seller account.

Option 1, if you are interested in only building and scaling your business, is to create the Amazon Seller account with the email and password from an existing Amazon Prime or regular account.

Option 2, if you are interested in building, scaling, and selling your business, is to create an Amazon Seller account with an email and password that are not yet associated with Amazon in any way. This will tremendously aid the brand transfer process by keeping your personal account and Seller account completely separate.

Next, Amazon is going to ask for your personal or business (if you have it) information. Fill out the documents they request such as your address, driver's license, and billing information, just to name a few. Remember to make sure that all of your personal information matches exactly, down to a middle initial on your license for example, across all types of identification.

Now, let's dive into some of the questions they may ask during the signup process. The first question they may ask is: **Do you have universal product codes for all of your products?**

The answer is a resounding "yes", but you may not have them yet. Don't worry, though, because when you list your product on Amazon, they will ask you for a UPC code. Every product has a barcode on it, and that barcode is the UPC code. You can buy these codes, and it's necessary for putting your product on Amazon. When you do this, Amazon will see your product as a brand-new product in their catalog.

The second question may sound confusing, but don't worry, the answer is straightforward. The question is, **"Are you the manufacturer for any of the products you want to sell on Amazon?"**

You're going to answer "yes" to this, even though you aren't actually the manufacturer. As a private labeller, you're working with manufacturers to create your products. However, in Amazon's eyes, you are the manufacturer because you'll be the only one manufacturing this product.

Finally, the last question they may ask is, **"Do you own government-registered trademarks of the brand products you'll be selling on Amazon?"**

If you don't have any trademarks registered yet, which is likely the case, you can answer "no". This is not a problem, and you can always register your trademarks later on.

YOUR ACTION STEP FOR TODAY

AMAZON ACCOUNT SETUP

Step 1: Navigate to Amazon.com and scroll down to the bottom. Click on "Sell products on Amazon".

Step 2: Scroll to the bottom of that webpage and click on "Sign up to become an individual seller".

Step 6: Sign up for an Amazon Seller account.

   a. Option one, if you are interested in only building and scaling your business, is to create the Amazon Seller account with the email and password from an existing Amazon Prime or regular account.

   b. Option two, if you are interested in building, scaling, and selling your business, is to create an Amazon Seller account with an email and password that are not yet associated with Amazon in any way. This will tremendously aid the brand transfer process by keeping your personal account and Seller account completely separate.

Step 4: Input various personal information such as your drivers license, banking information, phone number, and proof of address, just to name a few.

Step 5: Think of a storefront name (optional). You can always change it later.

Step 6: Amazon may need to verify your new account via telephone, Zoom call, or postcard.

Step 6: Once verified, your account is open and ready for you to start selling!

What would it be like for you if you could see money as a powerful tool for blessing others and building a better life for yourself and your loved ones?

It's interesting how people can have a double standard when it comes to making money. They'll say they want to be healthy, have a great marriage, and raise successful children. But when it comes to money, they often adopt a poverty mindset, saying they don't need too much. This mindset puzzles me, because money can be a powerful tool for changing your family's legacy and blessing others, especially when it's in the hands of people who use it wisely!

If you're still with us on Day 7 in this book, you're likely someone who sees money as a tool, not just to buy back your time, but also to build an asset for your family and bless others. Money is simply a tool for exchange, and people trade money for things they value. If building a passive income business, like the one we teach, is more valuable to you than keeping your money, then invest in yourself and join our program. We will help you get to the level you want to be at.

People often hesitate to invest in themselves because they believe they can't afford it. But in reality, we always buy what we want, not just what we can afford.

If you want to build a financially free lifestyle, a business that can scale without taking away from your family, then find a way to afford this program. You can't afford not to become a Rainmaker!

If you're wondering how to fund the mastermind and your inventory, we offer Rainmaker funding, where we're willing to finance you and put you on a payment plan.

Yet, investing in a program alone is not enough. Course completion stats show that only 12.9% of people who buy a course actually complete it. And even completing a course doesn't mean they take action. That's why we offer more than just a course. We offer a comprehensive system that includes coaching, community, and tools to help you move the needle in your business every day.

Our community provides daily coaching calls on specific topics such as product research, pre-launch, launching, and maintenance. Group Accelerator coaching is also available to help you with any questions you may have. In addition, we have software like the Move the Needle Tool, the Product Qualifier Tool, and the Power Profit Tool to help you overcome any pain points you may encounter.

Our Rainmaker Mastermind is more than just a course. It's a comprehensive system that takes you through the entire process of building a successful business. We listen to our Rainmakers and create solutions for any problems that may arise. Our community is full of people who will cheer you on, encourage you, and help you break through any walls you encounter!

If you're still hesitant and wondering what if this doesn't work, I challenge you to ask yourself, "What if it does work?" Where you focus matters, and by focusing on the abundance that's possible through this program, you can transform your life and your family's life. We're so confident in our program and the results it delivers that we don't offer a 30-day money-back guarantee, but our action-based $10k Payday Guarantee, where you make $10k, or we pay you $10k.

We reward decisiveness and commitment, and we believe that the money you invest in yourself will replenish and give you a return on your investment.

So, if you're ready to take the next step and join our community of Rainmakers, fill out an application at **www.rainmakerchallenges.com/apply**.

We carefully review applications and if we believe you're a good fit, we'll be in touch to help you get started!

YOUR DAY 7
QUICK WIN:

SETTING UP YOUR AMAZON SELLER ACCOUNT

Follow these simple steps:

1. Go to amazon.com, scroll to the bottom, and click on "Sell products on Amazon."
2. At the bottom of the next page, click on "Sign up to become an individual seller."
3. Follow the prompts to create your account and provide the needed personal or business information.
4. Once your account is verified, start listing your products!

Once you've set up your seller account, you'll be one step closer to achieving your financial freedom.

Have you submitted your Rainmakers application at **www.rainmakerchallenges.com/apply**?

Don't hesitate, take action today and start building your Amazon business with the help of our Rainmaker Mastermind community!

Rainmaker

#CELEBRATIONS

☂

Rainmaker Abby:

"I joined the Rainmaker Academy in February and learned that product research is crucial for success. It was challenging for me even though I have experience in clinical research. My coach was a lifesaver, and I saved a lot of money with his guidance!

One day, my messy boys gave me a brilliant product idea, a basketball hamper, and I immediately researched it on Helium 10. I fell in love with the tool and still use it every day to spy on the market and see what's working.

Product research is key, and I'm launching my hamper now after finding success with the right product.

Today, I received my first huge payment from Amazon, and even my husband is now on board with my business venture!"

12

DAY EIGHT: BEGINNER TO PRO – HELIUM 10 HACKS

What would it be like for you if you could find the perfect product to launch your business on Amazon?

One that fills a gap in the market, has existing demand, and is validated to be profitable?

Well, that's exactly what we're going to dive deeper into and help you with inside today's bonus chapter – **product research**!

Over the last seven days, we've laid a strong foundation, and if you've taken your next step to become a part of our Rainmaker Mastermind, you have unlocked access to extensive further training on product research.

Today, we're going to show you tips and strategies on how to find a product, including out-of-the-box methods and our top 10 tips for utilizing Helium 10.

Now, we want to be clear: finding products to sell on Amazon is not *easy*. Sure, some people might make it seem like a breeze, but it will take persistence and effort. Yet with the right tools and guidance, you can simplify this process and find YOUR "breakthrough products"!

The core of everything we're going to talk about today is finding that existing demand on Amazon and how to take advantage of it.

Having said that, you will also need to consider the competition. Just because there's high demand for collagen peptides or hand sanitizer, for example, doesn't mean it's the right product for you to sell. Established competition can make it difficult for new brands to break through.

So, we're going to balance finding that demand, with validating it to ensure it's a viable option for you. As the saying goes, *"so you're saying there's a chance?"* – we want to make sure that chance is **worth your time and effort**.

10 TIPS FOR UTILIZING HELIUM 10

Have you ever wondered how successful businesses come up with new product ideas that seem to capture the market's attention?

It's not always easy to know what products will be popular and profitable, but there are tools and strategies that can help. As mentioned in one of our previous chapters, one of the best tools out there is Helium 10.

If you're ready to start your Amazon business, you absolutely need to get Helium 10. Trust us, this tool is a game-changer. It can save you money, make you money, and it's going to help you out in your business in so many ways.

I know a lot of people start with Helium 10 for product research, but once you start using it, you'll realize there's a whole suite of tools inside that are going to take your Amazon business to the next level. Whether you're just starting out or looking to grow your business, Helium 10 can help you find new product opportunities and stay ahead of the competition.

So, here are our top 10 tips to help you get familiarized with Helium 10:

1. When you're doing product research on Amazon, it's important to **have a starting point**. You don't necessarily need a tool or anything to begin with, just an idea of what you want to sell.

2. One way to start is to type a keyword into Amazon and **look at the related searches at the bottom of the page**. Amazon suggests these related searches based on what people are actually searching for.

3. Once you find a keyword you're interested in, **check its search volume** and **look for related keywords** that have buyer intent.

4. When you're looking at search results, **pay attention to the first few products that come up**. If they're not directly related to your search term, it could mean there's little competition for your product idea.

5. Don't be intimidated by products with thousands of reviews. **Look for products with only a few reviews or even none at all**, as they could be new to the market and easier to compete with.

6. Use Helium 10 to **analyze the titles of products** that come up in search results. The "title density" metric can give you an idea of how often a keyword appears in the titles of top-ranking products. This can help you optimize your own product's title for search. Title density refers to the frequency of a keyword appearing in the titles of the top results on page one of Amazon search results. Knowing title density is essential because the ultimate goal is to rank on page one of the search results.

7. **Use one-click filters** to quickly gather insights when browsing through search results. For example, if you type in a keyword like "bunny," you can see the title density of related keywords such as "bunny toys," "bunny plushies," "bunny ears," and "bunny slippers". This information will give you an idea of how competitive the keyword is and whether you should consider it.

8. Competing products data is available on Helium 10, but it's not always necessary to worry about the number of competing products. Instead, you should **focus on who is on page one of the search results**. When the number of competing products is over 500, it is not that meaningful.

9. Helium 10 also provides data on related keywords, both before and after the keyword you entered. This information can lead you down the rabbit hole of discovering products you may not have considered before. **"Smart Complete Keywords" is a part of the Helium 10 Magnet Tool which** can help you in your research, bringing up a keyword or key phrase listed in Amazon's index that exactly matches the word or phrase you are searching for.

10. Finally, you can **see the countries of origin of the sellers for a particular keyword** on Helium 10. While some may be concerned about competing with foreign sellers, this information can also be advantageous. For example, if you are a German seller and you see that all the sellers in your niche are from the USA, you may have an advantage since you can create better listings in German than they can. However, you should also take the cost of the item and available margin into account, regardless of where the sellers are located.

COMMON HELIUM 10 FAQs

Q: How can I see the search volume graph on Helium 10?

A: You can see the search volume graph on Helium 10 by looking for a mini icon of a graph where you see "search volume." Clicking on it will display historical data.

Q: What is a good indicator of demand on Amazon?

A: To find product opportunities on Amazon, you need to find existing demand. A good indicator of demand is monthly revenue, which is a function of sales. **Look for products that sell at least 300 units per month and have a maximum of two sellers on the product**. You can also narrow your search by filtering for product categories, review count, and listing age.

Q: How many variations of a product should I start with?

A: It's best to **start with just one variation of a product** to avoid investing too much in a product that may not sell. As a newer product, you may not know which variation is the top seller, so it's better to test the waters with one before expanding.

Q: How is product research different when you want to max-imize a seasonal product, like a Christmas stocking stuffer gift or a candy corn box? Do you just look at the seasonal search volume?

A: When doing product research for a seasonal product, it's important to look at the historical data and search volume for that product to determine the level of demand. You can use tools like Helium 10 to look at the search volume graph and see when there are spikes in search volume. This will help you determine the seasonality of the product. It's also important to plan ahead and launch a little before the season to ride the wave up. If it's your first product, it may be best to avoid seasonal products to avoid the risk of miscalculations and excess inventory.

TOP FIVE HELIUM 10 TIPS

Tip 1: Look for the keywords that have buyer intent and that are very specific to a niche.

Tip 2: Search for trending products on Etsy & Pinterest and then double check the lifetime search volume for the keyword to check the potential longevity of the keyword.

Tip 3: If it is going to be your first time launching on Amazon, invest in single products instead of launching multiple variations

Tip 4: Product research takes time to learn so be kind to yourself and surround yourself with positive and encouraging people (The Rainmaker Family!).

Tip 5: Remember, the ultimate goal of product research is to find a niche product with low competition.

The most successful people in any field are the ones who are able to keep learning and keep growing. You don't have to be an expert, you don't have to have a lot of experience, you don't have to have a lot of money. All you need is a little bit of knowledge, a little bit of persistence, and a lot of hard work."

THE
Rainmaker
FAMILY

YOUR NEXT STEPS

Congratulations on completing this chapter, and kudos to you for taking the initiative to learn and grow your Amazon business! We hope you found today's Top 10 Helium 10 hacks for product research helpful and insightful.

As you continue on your journey towards financial freedom for yourself and your family, why stop here?

Why not take advantage of our Rainmaker Mastermind program to collapse time from where you are right now... and a profitable Amazon business that will allow you the time and financial freedom you desire for yourself and your family?

By joining our mastermind, you'll gain access to extensive training and support, including in-depth product research strategies, that will help you stay ahead of the competition and achieve your goals. Our community of 6 to 7-figure Amazon sellers and expert coaches are dedicated to helping you fast-track your business's growth and success!

So, if you're ready to turn your Amazon business dreams into reality and create the life you and your family deserve, we encourage you to submit your application to join our Rainmaker Mastermind today. Let's make your Amazon business a true success story together!

DAY 8

QUICK WIN:

BOOK YOUR FREE STRATEGY CALL WITH OUR TEAM

Imagine a life where your financial freedom is no longer a dream, but a reality...

Are you ready to take your next step towards creating a successful Amazon business?

If you are ready for your next step in accelerating your journey to the 6-figure and beyond Amazon business we've seen become a reality for so many of our Rainmakers, go to **www.rainmakerchallenges.com/apply** to submit your application and book your FREE breakthrough-unlocking call today!

Rainmaker

#CELEBRATIONS

Rainmaker Farah:

"Let me share an incredible journey with you. Initially, I had some doubts and hesitations, but I quickly realized that this process truly works. In just nine days, I sold 90 units of my product. Can you believe it? And within the first week, I made over $1,000, with a profit of around $800. It's incredible to see the tangible results so quickly.

For those of you who may be thinking, 'I don't have enough time for this,' I understand your concerns. As a busy person myself, I know how valuable every minute of the day is. But let me assure you, even if you can only dedicate a little bit of time each day or week, progress is possible. Challenges may arise, but with a 'How can I?' attitude and the support of the Rainmaker Mastermind community, you can overcome them.

Now, as I have been witnessing the success of my product, it's truly remarkable to receive constant notifications of sales, even when I'm spending quality time with my loved ones. I joined the challenge with a dream of building a small off-grid cabin to pass down to our generations and we were able to do just that! I earned enough from my one small product to buy land and build my dream cabin...enjoying every minute of it. Plus last year we were able to pay off our mortgage! The freedom that comes with being debt free is amazing!

So, I want to challenge you. If deep down, you feel the desire to pursue this opportunity, don't let doubt or fear hold you back. Trust that regardless of your schedule, you can make it happen. Results can exceed your expectations.

Take that leap of faith and join us on this incredible journey. The Rainmaker Mastermind is here to provide unwavering support and guidance every step of the way. Let's turn your dreams into reality together!"

13

DAY NINE: YOUR GRADUATION CEREMONY

Wow, we have reached the final chapter of our journey together in this book, and we want to celebrate your well-deserved graduation!

This moment is all about you, and we want to take a moment to recognize and honor your incredible achievement.

It's important to us that you understand the significance of the past nine days on your journey. You didn't just read this book; you immersed yourself in the material, absorbing every valuable insight and putting them into action through our quick wins.

By reaching this chapter, you have shown an extraordinary level of perseverance and a deep desire for the financial freedom of your family. It is evident that you are not just a reader, but a doer—a person who is willing to take the necessary steps to turn your dreams into reality!

If you've made the life-changing decision to step into our Rainmaker Mastermind community, we want to extend a warm and heartfelt welcome to you. You are now part of a vibrant and supportive group of like-minded individuals who are on a similar path of growth and success! This community is here to uplift and inspire you as you continue to push the boundaries of what you thought was possible.

You are now part of a collective force of Rainmakers, and we are honored to have you on this journey with us.

Embrace the momentum you have created and continue to forge ahead with confidence and determination! We are here to support you every step of the way, cheering you on and celebrating your victories. Your journey is just beginning, and we are excited to witness the incredible possibilities you will achieve.

THE RAINMAKER CHALLENGE

Graduation Diploma

THIS CERTIFIES THAT

has completed all the requirements of the curriculum
of the **Rainmaker Challenge** and is now qualified
to join the **Rainmaker Mastermind**

CHELSEY DIAZ
MAKE IT RAIN MAMA

STEPHEN DIAZ
PASSIVE INCOME PAPA

There are 3 special awards we give out inside of our Rainmaker Mastermind, and one of the reasons we love giving out these awards is because they symbolize the incredible progress and success that our Rainmakers have achieved!

Each award represents a significant milestone on their Amazon journey, from making their first $100 in a day to reaching six-figure sales and beyond. These milestones showcase the transformational power of the Rainmakers' dedication, determination, and unwavering belief in what's possible for them and their families.

Furthermore, these awards serve as tangible reminders of what is possible. They inspire our members to dream bigger, to set audacious goals, and to take intentional action that leads them to a next level of breakthrough. When a fellow Rainmaker receives an award, it sparks a fire within the hearts of others, igniting their desire to achieve similar feats. It creates a ripple effect of motivation and drives the entire community to push their boundaries and excel in their businesses!

And perhaps the most significant reason we love giving out these awards is the sense of unity and camaraderie they foster within our mastermind. The Rainmakers Mastermind is not just a collection of individuals; it's a tight-knit community of like-minded entrepreneurs who support, encourage, and uplift one another. When we celebrate the successes of our fellow Rainmakers, we reinforce the bonds that tie us together. We become cheerleaders, mentors, and friends united by a common purpose and shared journey.

So, here are the 3 awards you, too, can win, when you make the decision to keep the momentum you've built here going inside of our Rainmaker Mastermind. These are physical awards that you will receive in the mail and can be put in your home/office to remind you daily of what you've accomplished!

First, we have **the Benjamin Club Award**. Picture this: earning <u>your first $100 in a single day on Amazon</u>.... It may not sound like a fortune, but it's a powerful milestone that signifies your entry into the world of success. Imagine holding that golden $100 bill, a symbol of your hard work and determination. This award is all about celebrating your initial breakthroughs and setting the stage for bigger achievements to come!

Now, let's fast forward a bit. The next award on our list is **the Grand Rainmaker Award**. We're talking about consistently hitting <u>$1,000 in daily sales on Amazon</u>. It's a game-changer, our friend. Becoming a Grand Rainmaker means you've unlocked the secrets of scaling your business and created a whole new level of financial freedom. Imagine the excitement and pride that comes with reaching this milestone – you're part of an exclusive group of accomplished Rainmakers who have set their sights high and achieved extraordinary results!

But wait, there's more! The ultimate achievement is the **Six-Figure & Seven-Figure Family Awards**. Can you envision a life where <u>your annual sales exceed $100,000 or even $1,000,000</u>? Imagine the impact it would have on your family's financial well-being. On average at the time of writing this a new Rainmaker family gets our Six-Figure award every 14.2 days in our Mastermind community. Our vision is that in 10 years or less we have mama bears becoming millionaires EVERY day in our community. We just sent out two seven-figure awards for two families that crossed the $1M mark this week.

These major milestone awards represents the moment when your Amazon business becomes a powerful force, generating substantial income and opening doors to a world of possibilities. It's a powerful celebration moment that helps you reflect on who you had to become in the transformational process of building this business and it gives you fuel for long-term success.

As you reflect on these three incredible awards, we encourage you to take a moment to picture yourself as a recipient of each one.

Now, let's get real for a moment. These awards aren't just distant dreams or wishful thinking. They are within your reach, our friend. You've already absorbed the valuable insights and strategies shared in this book. You've shown dedication and a readiness for success.

It's time to take that leap and make these awards your reality!

Kendra
Top contributor · +1 · April 8

👏This is amazing!!! 👏

After only 1 month, we've just about reached Grand Rainmaker status!!! Only 1 sale away from reaching $1000 in ONE DAY!!! 🤞 (hopefully we can get one more by the end of today! 🤞)

This has been an amazing journey for us! 🖤🖤Couldn't have done it without my amazing coach Lainie ▒▒▒▒🙏 It has definitely been worth every effort!!

Mandy ░░░░
3d · 🌐

🎉 Celebrations Post 🎉

Hey y'all! Just wanted to jump on here and throw out some celebrations!! One to encourage our new friends and two to keep myself pushing to do even better!!

Started Rainmaker mastermind in Sept 2022. Launch was delayed by CNY and Covid shutdown at my factory but we launched our first product April 7, 2023! I hit my first (no giveaways) Benjamin club 💵 sales day on Day 9! Since then we have been steadily selling the past two months.

I... **See more**

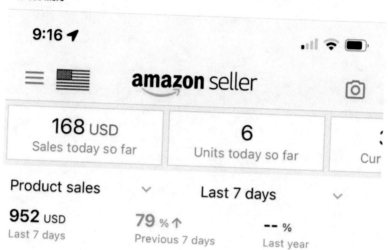

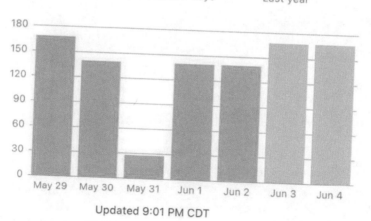

 **Tiffany**
May 31 at 5:19 PM · 🌐

6-figure family award! 🎉🎉

We launched 2 products 4.5 months ago. We had to restock in March and April (which is why there is a dip on our sales graph). We launched product 3 in May, and will launch product 4 in July. 🎉🎉

I'm so grateful for all of the tools this program has provided to me. Joining the Mastermind program was one of the best decisions I have made.

#c... **See more** — with **Steven**

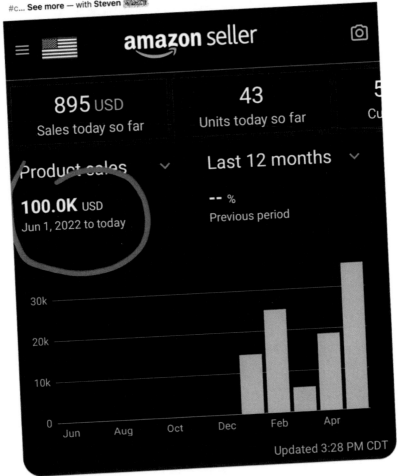

Rainmaker Mastermind Members Only // @TheRainmakerFamily   ···   ✕

Kourtnye ▓▓▓ · 44m · 🌐

Ahhh oh my goodness guys! I can't believe I'm actually holding this award! I NEVER in a million years would think I could ever build a million dollar business. We accomplished this last fall but just now getting to share. Since joining rainmakers I've added two babies to our family making us a family of seven! 👶 I honestly do very minimal in my business now as it almost feels like free money! The process does work! What a blessing this group has been to my family! Don't give up! If Stephen and Chelsey wouldn't have charged a decent amount for Mastermind I wouldn't have kept going. I'm sure I would have doubted myself and quit but because I knew I had so much invested I told myself I had to finish! What a blessing! Thank you Stephen Diaz and Chelsey Diaz for making this possible!

"It seems as though there is a hidden guide who's duty it is to test men through all sorts of discouraging experiences. Those who don't pass the persistence test, don't make the grade. Those who do, arrive at the top of the ladder and are bountifully rewarded for their persistence. They receive, as their compensation, whatever goal they are pursuing. But they receive something infinitely more; the knowledge that every failure carry's with it the seed of an equivalent advantage."

-Napoleon Hill

Huge milestone reached today! Many of you know me and have known of the challenges I've faced in my business. Many of you have heard my story on day 5 of the on demand challenge or from The Rainmaker Family Podcast.

I know some of you are struggling. I know that some of you have encountered discouraging situations that can seem to cripple your resolve, drain your passion and that can potentially induce debilitating discouragement...if you allow it. Being discouraged is natural, but I urge you to not give in to it. I urge you to find gratitude in the simple things in life, which are the most wonderful blessings God has poured out upon you and that have nothing to do with financial success.

I'm not sure I've known anyone in this group that has gone through the difficulties I have (even just a few days ago wiring $10k to settle a lawsuit and get it behind me) and I am here to encourage you to press forward no matter how intensely you are tested. There will be personal growth and success...I promise. Never give up, never give in...never EVER quit.

We launched our first product 18 months ago and in the past 12 months have reached $1M in revenue.

I was able to purchase my dream truck! I give all the glory and thanks to God for carrying me through difficult times and granting me the faith to continue!

#DailyWins — with Rebecca ▓▓▓▓▓▓▓▓▓▓▓▓▓ and 12 others.

⚠ Your account is at risk of deactivation

| 7465 USD | 234 | 1(|
| Sales today so far | Units today so far | Curr |

Product sales ⌄	Last 12 months ⌄
1.000M USD	229 % ↑
Jun 1, 2022 to today	Previous period

SOME FINAL WORDS OF
ENCOURAGEMENT FOR YOUR JOURNEY

As we come to the end of this chapter, we want to leave you with some heartfelt encouragement from our fellow Rainmakers.

We understand that you may be feeling a mix of excitement and nervousness as you step into this new territory of starting an Amazon business. If that resonates with you, let's hear from a few seasoned Rainmakers here as they reflect on their journeys and offer some valuable insights and encouragement:

Rainmaker Jasmine shares her perspective:

"When we have a reason behind what we do, it adds a whole new level of meaning and purpose. Think about all the times you've gone above and beyond for someone you love or care about without hesitation. Now, imagine applying that same mindset to yourself. Remember, you're not being selfish by embarking on this journey. You're doing it for your future, your family, and your children. There's nothing to lose and everything to gain. Envision looking back a year from now and reflecting on the choices you made today. Visualize the progress and growth you'll experience. Perhaps you'll be in your dream home or a beautiful vacation spot. Keep that vision in mind and focus on your why. When you look back, the journey will be worth it."

Rainmaker Amy Sharon says:

"When I discovered Rainmakers and showed my husband the possibilities,

everything changed. We made a deal: If I could launch a product on Amazon, we would reconsider baby number six." In November 2021, I launched my first product, and in November 2022, we joyfully welcomed our sixth child in the form of financial blessings. I want to remind you to focus on your why, to keep pushing forward, and to envision the incredible possibilities that lie ahead. Embrace the support of the Rainmaker community and never give up, even during the challenging moments."

Rainmaker Kathy shares her journey of overcoming fear and doubts. She says:

"Fear is not just a feeling but a spirit that seeks to hold us back. I realized that I needed to borrow Stephen's faith. He offered his faith to those who felt they lacked it, and I took him up on that offer.

You have the power within you to conquer fear and pursue your dreams. The Rainmaker community is a place of security and support. If you're on the fence, don't let fear stop you. Embrace the faith that's available to you.

Age and external opinions shouldn't hold you back from pursuing your dreams. Believe in yourself and know that the Rainmaker community is cheering you on every step of the way."

Rainmaker Kristi says:

"Imagine what your life could look like one year from today, two years from today. If you take this step it could be a hundred percent different than it is right now. The me before Rainmakers and the me now are in some ways, like two different people. I'm doing things now and thinking in ways now that I never thought were possible. I'm achieving goals and dreaming dreams that

I didn't even know I could. Rainmakers has given me so much hope for the future and I want that for you too. I just can't wait for you to join us."

14

ONE LAST MESSAGE FOR YOU!

As we come to the final pages of our book, we want you to know that as someone who has journeyed with us over the last 9 days and stayed till the very end - we wholeheartedly believe in you.

We see your potential, your unique gifts, and the incredible impact you can make in the world, and if you will allow us to, we are here to support you every step of the way, providing guidance, encouragement, and a community that believes in your success.

We invite you to share your wins and celebrate your achievements on the Rainmaker Challenge testimonial page at **www.rainmakerchallenges.com/booktestimonial**

Your story is powerful, and by sharing it, you inspire others to embark on their own transformative journeys. Your voice matters and your experiences have the potential to uplift and encourage those who may be walking a similar path.

If you are ready to take the next step, we encourage you to **explore the possibility of joining our 12-month Rainmaker Mastermind program**.

Within this exclusive community, you will find a network of like-minded individuals who are committed to securing their family's freedom and creating extraordinary results through their Amazon businesses. It is a space where you can continue to learn, grow, and receive the support and accountability needed to reach new heights.

Imagine the possibilities that await you as a Rainmaker... Picture yourself, just months from now, proudly joining our Benjamin Club. The sense of accomplishment, the financial freedom, and the limitless potential that comes with it. What would that be worth to you? For some, it would be priceless.

We understand that investing in yourself may seem daunting, but it's important to shift your perspective. This is not a mere cost; it is an investment in your future, a trade of dollars for a specific result. Think about it: people willingly invest in business franchises, often waiting years before seeing any profit. They pay exorbitant amounts for prestigious universities, knowing that their income may not match the investment. Yet, they fail to recognize the immense value of the coaching industry.

Don't fall into the trap of believing you can't afford to become a Rainmaker. Challenge yourself to think differently. **Ask, "How can I afford this?"**

The truth is, you can't afford not to afford it. The cost of staying stuck, financially and emotionally, far outweighs the investment you make today. Our Rainmaker Mastermind is not a fleeting opportunity; it is a real business that can be built, scaled, and even sold for a seven-figure exit in just a few short years.

Consider the steps you've already taken. You've invested in Helium 10, dedicating time and energy to learn and grow. You've spent nine valuable days with us, demonstrating your commitment and determination. You know your "why" and have a burning desire to succeed.

Now, imagine cultivating a tree that bears fruit, each fruit containing more seeds. With our Rainmaker Mastermind, you have the power to create flourishing orchards, provide for your own family, create job opportunities, and making a profound impact on the world.

Don't let the fear of investment hold you back. Embrace the belief that your dreams are worth pursuing, and that the rewards will far surpass the initial investment. Unlock the secrets of unlimited wealth and financial freedom. Become a Rainmaker and witness the transformative power it holds for years to come.

The choice is yours, and we challenge you to choose abundance, growth, and a future filled with possibility!

With heartfelt appreciation and unwavering belief in your potential,

Stephen & Chelsey

YOUR NEXT
QUICK WIN:

CONTINUE YOUR RAINMAKER JOURNEY WITH US INSIDE OF OUR 12-MONTH MASTERMIND

Congratulations on completing this incredible journey with us! As you reach the final pages of this book, we want to leave you with a vision of the extraordinary life that awaits you as a Rainmaker.

Imagine a life where financial freedom is not just a distant dream, but a tangible reality. A life where you have the power to create a successful business, that provides the lifestyle for your family that you've always desired. If you're feeling trapped in your current circumstances, yearning for something more, it's time to take action.

Take the first step towards your transformative journey by submitting your Rainmaker Mastermind application at **www.rainmakerchallenges.com/apply**. By joining our exclusive Rainmaker Mastermind, you'll gain access to a community of like-minded individuals, expert coaches, and the tools necessary to turn your dreams into a thriving Amazon business.

We understand that the path to success may seem overwhelming at times, especially when it comes to financing your business. That's why we invite you to have a conversation with our dedicated team who is ready to assist you in finding creative solutions to fund your journey, ensuring that financial constraints don't hold you back.

It's natural to feel a hint of fear as you embark on this new chapter of your life... But remember, fear is simply a temporary barrier that can be overcome. Take the leap of faith, join us today, and let's work together to turn your Amazon business goals into a vibrant reality!

Thank you for being a part of our Rainmaker family. We believe that you are capable and will attain extraordinary transformation along your journey. We can't wait to witness the incredible heights you'll reach as a Rainmaker!

Your journey is just beginning, and the possibilities are endless. Embrace the path ahead with confidence and determination, knowing that if you so decide, you can have the unwavering support of a community dedicated to your success.

Dream big, take action, and let's make your Amazon business dreams a living, breathing testament to what's possible with unwavering dedication and passion.

The world is waiting for your Rainmaker legacy. We look forward to seeing you on the inside of our Mastermind!

Nicole DeFelice

After serving in Afghanistan I promised myself that I would never miss another moment with my children. Rainmakers came into my life like a shooting star to answer my prayers. At the height of the pandemic, I dove into creating an Amazon FBA business and six months later I launched my first product on Amazon. Since then, I've launched two more products and plan to continue working towards a seven-figure exit. Thanks to Rainmakers we purchased an RV and are making lifelong memories traveling!

Cyndy Keene

I began Feb 2020. I was all in. An item ready to order & then my house burnt down. When I returned, numbers changes & the item wasn't going to work. I was depressed & quit. A bit later I was in the mastermind group & saw a video that brought me back. After a quick call with my coach, I knew this is where God wanted me. I have now figured out my brand, product line & have plant to retire in 2 years thanks to my Rainmaker journey I am now living. my best life & blesssings keep coming.

Cassie Ford

Prior to joining Rainmakers, I was a nurse that worked at least 3 12-hour shifts a week and missed lots of moments with my family. I found Rainmakers while searching for other ways to make money during my maternity leave! At the end of the challenge, I knew my life would never be the same. I launched 2 products my first year and have seen tremendous success! I have taken this step into entrepreneurship with a full and expectant heart and cannot wait to see how Belle Packs will continue to grow!

Jasmyn Young

I joined Rainmakers October 1, 2020. One year later I launched my first gateway product. Before Rainmakers I never imagined I could become an e-Commerce seller. Rainmakers provided a village of loving, driven, like-minded entrepreneurs and leaders. So many breakthroughs in mindset and visions. I wanted to inspires my children and create a legacy. Already a self-made multi millionaire in real estate and now equipped with the tools to pursue my first million with Amazon. Thank you Stephen and Chelsey.

Melissa Benson

I has been praying for financial breakthrough for 2-1/2 years when I discovered Rainmakers. I knew really quickly that it was going to be the thing that helped shift the landscape of our family's financial future. 11 months after the launch of our first products, we hit $100K in sales. We are currently building a brand/business we one day plan to sell for millions. Being a Rainmaker has been instrumental in my growth as an entrepreneur, opening countless doors and helping propel me into my destiny.

We believe in community over competition. Our number one mission is to support our community of Rainmakers in building the life they want for their families.

Thanks to Rainmakers, we are hoping to hit 1 million in sales by the end of the summer.

I found Rainmakers in February of 2020! In that time I have launched two products and have had roughly $700,000 in sales - even with being out of stock almost 8 combined months of one year. Never would I have believed you if you had told me that a stay-at-home mom of 4 young boys could do this on her own, but somehow I did and I couldn't be more thankful for Rainmakers to give me the opportunity! We are hoping to hit 1 million in sales by the end of the 2022 summer!

- Kourtnye Siefker.

I'm a proud mompreneur of two successful Amazon FBA business babies!

Hi, my name is Kimberly and I'm a recovering serial entrepreneur. Before joining Rainmakers I had more business ventures than I could count on both hands. I was passionate about each of them, for a minute, then the fire would completely fizzle out once I did all the hard work just to see red on the bottom line. Now, I'm a proud mompreneur of two successful Amazon FBA business babies! It's only October and they have already made (in profit) double what my husband has at his current job!

- Kimberly Remedies.

From struggling with a failed Etsy shop to product LIVE & successful on Amazon

Before I joined Rainmakers, I was struggling with a failed Etsy shop and a general "feeling like a failure" mentality.
I knew I was meant to be a entrepreneur and that there was something in my life to do business and create streams of income.
Rainmakers helped me see a path forward and to take on the attitude of "how can I" in order to take concrete action and face walls and challenges I could have never anticipated I'd overcome!

- Joy B.

The future no longer looks dim to me, I can't wait to see what it holds.

As a 30 year old single-mom of one with an often debilitating mental illness, life had not positioned me in an advantageous position in June of 2020. That's when I discovered the Rainmaker Family. I adopted Stephen and Chelsey's,"How Can I?" mindset instead of believing, "I can't," and learned how to recognize opportunity everywhere. Since then I've launched my own brand with 2 products on Amazon and more to come. The future no longer looks dim to me-- I can't wait to see what it holds.

- Heidi Boles.

We were blown away by the impact this had on our family!

Our Rainmaker journey started on the mission field in Latin America. We were a full time missionary family for over 10 years and in desperate need for a financial breakthrough. We launched our first product on Amazon in October 2019. By October 2020 we had launched 4 more products and our business hit the 6-figure mark. We were blown away by the impact this had on our family, finances, and on me as a mom of 7 turned Boss Lady on e-Commerce. We are forever grateful to our RM family!

- Melissa Mejia.

I get to create my world exactly as I want it. Experience the Freedom I didn't know existed.

Before Rainmakers, I was trying to find my way in the entrepreneurial world, but nothing I tried felt fully mine nor did it meld into my family life exactly as I needed it to.
Now, I feel so fortunate that my business works when I can and want it to. I can give it as much or as little as I need in any given season of life and still be growing. That's a freedom I didn't know existed. I am still striving for my life, my business, and our dreams. I get to create my world exactly as I want it.

- Meredith Prater.

I've replaced my income and now never miss a beat with my kids.

Rainmakers changed our life for the better in so many ways! Before Rainmakers I owned and operated an independent hair salon. I missed out on all my kids practices and events. I worked nights and weekends to avoid daycare fees while my husband worked days. Fast forward a year & I've replaced my income and now never miss a beat with my kids. I'm even able to volunteer my time at Church and School because I stopped trading my time for money. Rainmakers has been one of our many, many blessings.

- Kayla Seidl.

I have launched 2 products so far and am on track to make more money this year than I did working as a nurse.

I joined the Rainmaker Academy almost one year ago, and I can honestly say it is one of the best decisions I have ever made! I have worked as a nurse for the past 9 years and have 3 young kids. I'd always dreamed of being a stay-at-home mom but financially, it just wasn't ever going to work out for us. I have launched 2 products so far and am on track to make more money this year than I did working as a nurse, all while now staying home with my kids!

- Rayna Johnson.

I've launched 3 products and my family is more financially stable today than I thought was possible.

Late 2019, I was forced out of a job I loved. I was broken and helpless. I knew I wanted to spend more time with then 3-year-old daughter and build a legacy for her, but I was unemployed and broke. Then the pandemic hit. 1-income family drowning in bills, and there was no light at the end of the tunnel. With a leap of faith, I joined the RM family and invested all my savings in my first product. I've launched 3 products and my family is more financially stable today than I thought was possible.

- Chidi Paige.

Cyndy ▮▮▮▮▮▮
Yesterday at 11:24 PM · ⊙   ···

#celebrations. Just hit 10k in sales since end of February launch!!!!

GET STARTED NOW

www.rainmakerchallenges.com/apply

RESOURCES

Watch the recorded video version of this challenge now at

www.rainmakerchallenges.com/book

ABOUT THE AUTHORS

Chelsey and her husband Stephen Diaz are the founders of The Rainmaker Family, where they create transformational experiences for moms who want to step into time freedom, generational abundance & leave a thriving family legacy. They do this primarily through what they call The Rainmaker Method, which is a four step process to help any family go from zero ideas, to launching an 7-Figure ecommerce brand online.

For years, Chelsey and Stephen ran a photography business in the wedding industry. One year they found themselves working 80 hour weeks, never having time for friends or family. They found themselves burnt out and overextended. It was that year they started exploring what income could look like for their family if they had more time leverage and time freedom.

They stumbled upon a little known program that Amazon runs that would pay them every two weeks, simply to supply in-demand products to the warehouses. They jumped on the opportunity and quickly scaled their Amazon "side hustle" into a full on business that replaced and retired them out of the wedding industry forever.

Chelsey and Stephen have gone on to share The Rainmaker Method for other families who want to get out of the hustle hamster wheel of trading dollars for hours.

Increasing leverage is the main focus of the program as they help moms avoid falling into "hustle traps" and learn to work from a place of rest. This transforms them into a rockstar CEO while still empowering them to raise world changers and leave a legacy. To do this, they leverage systems like Amazon FBA (fulfillment by Amazon) so that sales and shipping can happen in a hands-off way allowing any mom to scale her business without hiring a huge team or doing all the work herself.

FUTURE GOALS

Chelsey and Stephen Diaz are driven by impact and are on mission to become the #1 transformational personal development experience for moms to find purpose and profit working freely from home (or wherever) with a business they call their own. They are in the process of launching a venture capital fund for accredited investors who want to deploy private equity into upward trending women-owned ecommerce brands. (think shark tank for moms!)

The ultimate goal with the fund is to create a win-win scenario for both investor and brand owner. The Rainmaker Family will lean in with their own systems and team to scale and sell those brands producing not only generational wealth for the brand owner, but also passive income for investors with a potential big payout upon the successful exit of the brand. Chelsey Diaz always says "give a mom time freedom and financial freedom and she'll change the world" and The Rainmaker Family is excited to see how the launch of this fund will impact many more lives in their community.

*Focus on **what you have**, many major things start small.*
*The seeds you sow **will grow**.*
Sometimes you just gotta go before you know...

Made in the USA
Columbia, SC
30 October 2023

85670687-bee5-4454-93ea-b481f5635433R01